Washington
on
Washington

Washington
on
Washington

Edited by Paul M. Zall

THE UNIVERSITY PRESS OF KENTUCKY

Publication of this volume was made possible in part by a grant from the National Endowment for the Humanities.

Scholarly publisher for the Commonwealth,
serving Bellarmine University, Berea College, Centre College of Kentucky, Eastern Kentucky University, The Filson Historical Society, Georgetown College, Kentucky Historical Society, Kentucky State University, Morehead State University, Murray State University, Northern Kentucky University, Transylvania University, University of Kentucky, University of Louisville, and Western Kentucky University.

Editorial and Sales Offices: The University Press of Kentucky
663 South Limestone Street, Lexington, Kentucky 40508-4008

07 06 05 04 03   5 4 3 2 1

Frontispiece: Gilbert Stuart's *George Washington*. Courtesy of the Huntington Library, Art Collections, and Botanical Gardens, San Marino, California.

Library of Congress Cataloging-in-Publication Data

Washington, George, 1732-1799.
Washington on Washington / [compiled by] Paul M. Zall.
   p. cm.
Includes bibliographical references and index.
   ISBN 0-8131-2269-4 (Cloth : alk. paper)
   1. Washington, George, 1732-1799. 2. Presidents—United States—
Biography. 3. United States—Politics and government—1775-1783—
Sources. 4. United States—Politics and government—1783-1809—Sources.
5. Washington, George, 1732-1799—Archives. 6. Washington, George,
1732-1799—Quotations. I. Zall, Paul M. II. Title.
   E312.79.W3175 2003
   973.4'1'092—dc21   2002156189

FOR JAN MARION ZALL

CONTENTS

Introduction

GEORGE WASHINGTON'S SOCRATIC STYLE

In trying to assess George Washington's personality, the difficulty is distinguishing between the way we see him and the way he saw himself. The difference may be inferred from passages that talk about himself in his own writings, both public and private. The public statements fit the Olympian image of Washington in the national memory. The private statements in his journals and letters sometimes reveal a different person—one who will overflow with romantic feelings or wallow in sentimentality or explode with spontaneous wit, even in the privacy of a diary.

A quintessentially private person, Washington had a natural reluctance to express his feelings at all, a reluctance that was reinforced when his words were published to public scorn. He would be known by deeds, not words, but the written words remain to mirror him, often obliquely.

His public personality rose to the nation's needs for a military demigod subservient to civil authority and a president above party or special interest. But Washington's private personality surfaced when he retired to cultivate his gardens—relinquishing both military and political power more fit for a king.

In his public letter of 1783 announcing his military retirement and again a dozen years later in his celebrated Farewell Address, Washington urged his countrymen to set aside selfish regional interests for the sake of national unity. His prescription was to imitate Christ's "charity, humility and pacific temper of mind,"[1] a model shared by his old friend Benjamin Franklin.

When Franklin first learned that he was looked upon as a proud person, he adopted a regimen of daily exercises in humility. His prescription was to "imitate Jesus and Socrates,"[2] by which he meant cultivating humility in reality and appearance. To the former he attributed his reputation for integrity, to the latter his success in public councils.

Washington could have said the same. In an age when "politics" meant "crafty and cunning," he sustained public confidence by relying on rules of propriety to balance the appearance of Christian humility and the practice of Socratic detachment. This meant suppressing, in public at least, the "conviviality" and "humorous observations"[3] natural to him.

John Adams called him "the best actor of presidency we have ever had."[4] Thomas Jefferson said that Washington hated the ceremony of the office but played up to the public's expectations of it.[5] Abigail Adams marveled at the way he could balance the opposite and discordant "dignity that forbids familiarity" with the "easy affibility which creates Love and Reverence."[6] Even British observers wondered at his Socratic art of "concealing his own sentiments and of discovering . . . those of other men."[7]

In 1770, interested in acquiring more Western properties, Washington asked his younger brother Charles to scout the territory: "I should be glad if you would (in a joking way, rather than in earnest at first) see what value they seem to set upon their Lands."[8] All's fair in land speculating and war. On Long Island, he led even our side to believe the army was three times its actual size, leading to laments that a mere twenty thousand British regulars defeated sixty thousand Yanks.[9]

His grand, theatrical gestures seem out of place in Washington's behavior. In forming the army in 1776, he hoisted a "Great or Grand Union Flag." This was nothing but Great Britain's Meteor Flag modified with six horizontal stripes, but the new commander-in-chief made a great show by fluttering it on a fresh, seventy-six-foot flagstaff atop Somerville's Prospect Hill.[10] Nearing war's end, he dug with his own hands into the soil of Yorktown to signify the start of the siege, and once both French and American cannon were emplaced, he fired the first round.[11]

This sort of behavior conforms to the romantic sensibility that led to his notoriety in the 1750s. After killing a French officer alleged to have been an unarmed ambassador he confessed to having "assassinated" him, signing the document in French that he could not read—"The most infamous a British Subject ever put his Hand to."[12]

Compounding that misstep, which some still take as triggering the French and Indian War, Washington sent his brother a letter celebrating the delights of battle: "I heard Bullets whistle and believe me there was something charming in the sound."[13] The French intercepted the letter and subsequently published it throughout the Western world. The remark led George II to remark, "He would not say so, if he had been used to hear many."[14]

Twenty years later, in 1775, when someone asked if he had actually made that foolish statement, Washington answered, "If I said so, it was when I was young."[15] When the same kind of impetuous remarks surface in his later years, we are left to wonder how much represents the romantic overflow of powerful feelings and how much represents Socratic dissembling for fun, profit, or power.

For example, how are we to take the celebrated promise he is supposed to have made to the Virginia Convention in the Revolution's earliest days: "I will raise 1000 Men, subsist them at my own Expence, and march my self at their Head for the relief of Boston"?[16] That hearsay was reported by John Adams to show how Southerners had promoted Washington's candidacy to head the colonial army.

More theatrical was the incident towards the close of the war when Washington cooled the threat of mutiny among officers at Newburgh. He fumbled with his glasses while murmuring so all could hear, "I have not only grown grey but almost blind in the service of my country."[17] In a comparable incident at the war's end, he bid farewell to officers in New York. Impulsively he embraced each one by rank, from rotund Henry Knox on down, while "tears of deep sensibility filled every eye."[18]

And, as an example of his Christian humility, on the way to Mount Vernon, caught in a downpour, he is supposed to have left his horse for the common stage. When the coach stopped at a tavern the innkeeper invited the General to the private parlor, but Washington protested: "No, no. . . . It is customary for the people who travel in this stage always to eat together. I will not desert my companions."[19]

The seeming spontaneity of such gestures makes them credible, but sometimes the veneer cracks. An instance would be the episode in which Washington asked David Humphreys, familiar with European ritual, to arrange for the president's first formal reception. As they did in France, Humphreys stood by the door and, as Washington entered, bellowed, "The President of the United States!"—to a room with only five or six persons present.[20] Washington's response? "Well, you have taken me in once, but by God you shall never take me in a second time."[21]

Just as credible, because evident also in his writings, Washington's stony countenance could dissolve before "an unaffected sally of wit."[22] Congress excused its failure to provide funds because treasurer Robert Morris had his hands full. Washington replied that he wished Morris had his pockets full.[23] When Mrs. Washington chided him for saying grace before dinner with a clergyman at the table, Washington pardoned himself: "The reverend gentleman will at least be assured that at Mount Vernon we are not entirely graceless."[24]

At times, too, he would indulge guests with tall tales. He told a British visitor that the mosquitoes near Lake Champlain could bite through army boots.[25] He told a Boston merchant that the toads of Mount Vernon lit up at night from eating fireflies.[26] He would relate these stretchers with a quaint archness, barely suppressing a smile, a straightfaced performance in the Socratic mode.[27]

Natural versus contrived wit bubbles up in writing meant for his eyes only, as in docketing a begging letter from total stranger Thomas Bruff, who claimed to have had a vision that required five hundred pounds to fulfill. Washington docketed that letter, "From Mr. Thomas Bruff—without date and without Success."[28] His diary has such entries as the one recording a Sunday service in York, Pennsylvania. The town lacked an Episcopalian preacher, so Washington attended a Pennsylvania Dutch Reformed church. Since the service was in German and he had understood not a word, he reassured the diary, he had not been converted.[29]

Private correspondence also reveals the Washington wit. Former neighbor Eliza Powel writes from Philadelphia that the desk he had left behind had a secret drawer containing love letters. He replies that if she had found warmth in those letters, she must have set them afire.[30] And though he clearly preferred epigrammatic one-liners, he could join his aides in concocting elaborate jokes. Enticing women to dine at officers' mess, he included news of the cook's discovery that apples can be baked into pies.[31]

The higher he rose in public esteem, the more he guarded against such low laughter. The higher he ascended to secular sainthood, the more he had to guard against any public laughter at all.

Within a year after having nominated Washington commander-in-chief of the continental army, John Adams scolded Congress for idolizing "an image which their own hands have molten."[32] Before the fighting ceased, one Philadelphia newspaper was calling him "the Saviour of His Country," while a rival was urging readers, "Let us not make a God of him! It must give him pain, and cause him to blush."[33] The nation was demanding a demigod to compensate for the divine-right ruler they had shed.

Demand for his portraits required him to sit at least forty-six times, until (as he said) he felt like a trained horse who sat at the sight of a painter's brush.[34] He also suffered the pain of being plastered for a bust by American Joseph Wright and the more celebrated bust by French sculptor Jean Antoine Houdon—the first of which shattered when a workman dropped it and had to be redone.[35]

Washington made such sacrifices willingly, believing that the public represented the pivot upon which the mainspring of the new government must turn.[36] Madison observed that, without "idolizing public opinion, no man could be more attentive to the means for ascertaining it," approaching major political issues as if military campaigns.

"He spared no pains to gain information from all quarters; freely asking from all whom he held in esteem . . . a free communication of their sentiments," then making up his own mind.[37]

As a consequence, nobody acquired a better feeling for the national temper or enjoyed more popularity among all classes of people, the ignorant or uneducated, as well as "clever people, or those passing for such."[38] During the Constitutional Convention of 1787, when someone dropped a copy of the secret minutes, presiding officer Washington pocketed the paper until time to adjourn. Then he solemnly announced, "I know not whose Paper it is, but there it is (throwing it down on the table), let him who owns it take it"—and no one did.[39]

Outside the Convention hall, Washington's very presence dominated the scene. Crowds followed him on excursions to neighboring factories and foundries, as well as on fishing trips up the Delaware. His nostalgic return to Valley Forge, to revisit the site of that miserable camp from a decade before, formed a sort of triumphal procession for local citizens. July Fourth gave the press more excuse for lavish praise as "Ornament of all Virtue," "Terror of Depraved Men," and "First Among the Greatest."[40]

Speaking at the Convention only to urge closure, Washington played the role of scrupulously impartial presiding officer. His very presence influenced decisions. Pierce Butler said that in devising the presidency, delegates endowed the office with more powers than they actually intended simply because they had the model before them.[41]

While the journey to New York for the inauguration looked like the triumphal march of a monarch, he felt more as if being hauled to his hanging.[42] Sensitive to public expectations, however, he suffered himself to exchange his carriage for a white horse before a grand entrance into Philadelphia and put up with an orgy of public receptions en route.[43] Embarking on a crimson carpet from a barge rowed by thirteen pilots and escorted by a school of porpoises, he graciously accepted a military escort this time but vowed that in the future he would depend for safety on the American people.[44]

Even cynics marveled at his bearing. His natural dignity defied description. Sir James Bland Burges saw him as "cold, reserved, and even phlegmatic without the least appearance of haughtiness or ill nature," with an odd compound of pride and "constitutional diffidence."[45]

He captivated Congress. After agreeing to reply to his presidential address in a body, they conceded that walking would "not have comported with the dignity and splendor" of the occasion, and so they ransacked the city's livery stables for carriages suited to a royal address from the throne.[46]

Their enthusiasm reflected the problem Washington faced in reconciling the rhetoric of democracy with the ritual of monarchy. Lacking precedent, his inauguration imitated the coronation of George the Third. Even old Roger Sherman was said to have tried to devise "some style of address more novel and dignified than 'excellency.'"[47]

Washington was aware of the problem: "There is scarcely any part of my conduct which may not hereafter be drawn into precedent."[48] He asked Madison, as Congressional leader, and his Cabinet to submit their ideas on how to conduct the office. "Many things," he said, "which appear of little importance in themselves and at the beginning, may have great and durable consequences."[49] He polled them on whether he ought to tour the states as a means of studying regional people, places, and issues—a practice Jefferson discarded in his term as publicity seeking.[50]

Respecting the dignity of the office, he walked a fine line between high living and splendor appropriate to a democracy, as when sending his staff to find "a sett of those waiters or salvers, or whatever they are called," ornamenting the tables of wealthy Philadelphians and foreign ambassadors.[51] In contrast, he thrice rejected designs for coins because they bore his likeness.[52] Diehard democrats complained about his elegant carriage with six horses, four servants, and a quartet of escorts, but Abigail Adams said he ought to have more "state," not less.[53]

At the same time, she saw the risk: "If he was not really one of the best intentioned men in the world, he might be a very dangerous one."[54] The possibility gave antagonists the opening they needed for criticizing monarchical ritual. Complaints in the press rumbled about celebrating Washington's birthdays, swelled following the elaborate festivities for the second inaugural, and burst repeatedly after his proclamation of neutrality in the war between Britain and France, his leading troops against whiskey rioters, and worst of all, his sponsoring the Jay treaty favoring Britain.[55]

Jefferson recorded the president's "much inflamed" reaction: "*By god,* he had rather be in his grave than in his present situation. That he had rather be on his farm than to be made *emperor of the world* and yet they were charging him with wanting to be a king."[56]

And when even an old friend like Edmund Randolph criticized him in print, he put aside all pretense of being impervious to criticism. Visitor James Ross found the ladies of the family in great alarm. The president entered the parlor, his face "dark and lowering." Someone asked if he had read Randolph's pamphlet, *Vindication* (1795). "I have," said Washington, "and, by the eternal God, he is the damnedest liar on the face of the earth!" he exclaimed as he slammed his fist down upon the table.[57]

Such explosions in private provide a measure of the control he imposed upon himself in public. He tried to be magnanimous in both the Christian sense of being "great souled" and the classical sense of believing he deserved great merit and in fact being worthy of it.

Some would say his response to the Whiskey Rebellion was an overreaction to a local riot, forgetting that the memory of Shays' Rebellion that seized a federal armory must have reinforced the decision for swift, sharp action. That reaction reassured the nation and the watching world that President Washington was in control.

He blamed national unrest on radical Democratic Societies and the Francophile press. John Jay had counseled against name-calling as damaging to the president's "dignity and authority," but Washington could have replied that the results justified the meanness.[58]

He made no secret of blaming the whiskey riots on the Societies. Preparing a final report to Congress, he said he wished to be "more prolix" than usual rather than let the report, "go naked into the world, to be dressed up according to the fancy or the inclination of readers, or the policy of our enemies."[59]

Madison, warning that the attack would undercut his role as nonpartisan president, said it was "the greatest error" of Washington's political life.[60] He could no longer claim to be above party, and worse, his partisans would make political capital by stifling dissent of any kind under cover of protecting the president from "artful and designing men."

That was the term Washington had used against those who would sow seeds of jealousy and distrust on the streets

and in the press, weakening "the best fabric of human government and happiness, that has ever been presented for
the acceptance of mankind"[61]—a slogan recurring until the
close of his term.

In attacking "Mob and Club Government," he returned
often to the theme of his own personal sacrifices, opening
himself to personal attack. He reassured Henry Lee that no
critic could be more anxious "to put me aside than I am to
sink into the profoundest retirement."[62] But Garritt Minor,
for one, who disagreed with Washington's principles and
acts as "improper, erroneous and subversive of our liberties . . . never impeached the purity or goodness of his
heart."[63]

Washington just as gradually came to suspect critics as
a conspiracy among the "many hot heads and impetuous
spirits among us" energized by "the malignancy of the discontented, the turbulent, and the vicious."[64] When John Jay
returned from England to face violent public reaction, he
reassured the president that he expected "factious evils" as
phenomena no less natural than whirlwinds and meteors.[65]
Washington concurred but saw them less charitably as dregs
that "will always remain and the slightest motion will stir
them up."[66]

Hypersensitivity to public criticism affected even his
domestic life. When the Washingtons wished to provide a
refuge for Lafayette's exiled son, they lodged him separately
and secretly. Opposition congressmen, discovering the secret, opened an official inquiry to embarrass Washington
for not taking the youth into the president's own home.
His supporters insisted the secrecy was from "that noble
generosity which delights in dispensing charity in Secret,"[67]
but he confessed to Senator George Cabot that the secrecy
was to forestall Francophile criticism.[68]

Various drafts of Washington's Farewell Address offer the clearest sign of how deeply criticism had weakened his once solid reliance on the appearance of being a proper, dispassionate public servant. The address, composed for newspaper publication to moderate the fury of party spirit, warned against foreign intrigue and pseudopatriots intent on eroding public confidence in the presidency and ultimately the American form of government itself.

Washington named Madison as one who knew very well of his wish to relinquish the office at the close of his first term. The draft opened with a half-dozen paragraphs Madison had composed for him a few years earlier, then Washington added nine wishes of his own for a stronger union. He wound up with a remarkable flight of "egotisms," denying what he was affirming—that he would not notice "such virulent abuse" as the press had inflicted on his reputation and feelings. He concluded with a no less remarkable apologia for his conduct in office, reacting directly to charges in the press that he had profited financially from the presidency.[69]

Although insisting that his "politicks have been unconcealed—plain and direct," he nevertheless asked Hamilton to clothe the rough draft in "an honest, unaffected simple garb" with "egotisms" removed—adding, "however just they may be."[70] He also asked for removal of "personalities . . . allusions to particular measures," and especially "expressions which could not fail to draw upon me attacks which I should wish to avoid, and might not find agreeable to repel."

Hamilton's revision transformed the original self-pitying apologia into a dignified, statesmanlike assessment of Washington's principles and policy. This would be expected, since Hamilton still led the Federalists in or out of the Cabinet. But he also tempered Washington's tone, especially where the president himself had indicated in the margin, "the imputation of affected modesty" or "the appearance of self-distrust and mere vanity,"[71] evidence—if more were needed—that he was still trying to live up to the image expected of him as democratic demigod, passionate patriot, dispassionate president, rising superior over the shocks and injuries of fortune.

He continued to ask friends to look over his official correspondence with as critical an eye as the opposition press would do, hoping thereby to blunt criticism. But the Farewell Address taunted "ambitious, corrupted, or deluded citizens" who would betray their country while cloaking themselves in "a commendable deference for public opinion."

They refocused their attacks on Washington's ill-tempered "egotisms" as "the loathings of a sick mind."[72] Benjamin Franklin Bache's *Aurora* said, "If ever a nation was debauched by a man, the American Nation has been debauched by Washington."[73] Their aim, said William Duane, echoing John Adams in 1777, was to "Expose the PERSONAL IDOLATRY into which we have been heedlessly running."[74]

Despite such hysterical reactions to the Farewell Address, the idolatry flourished. Visitors from abroad noted how Washington enjoyed the respect of all classes, how he seemed "an emanation from the Omnipotent," how "every American considers it his sacred duty to have [his] likeness in his home" as if an image of God's saints.[75]

Upon relinquishing the office, at last he could reassume the low profile he preferred. At John Adams's inauguration, in his dark suit, he insisted that the new president precede him through the doorway. But dismissing the glory from his own head had become impossible. An entire generation had grown up under his paternal eye, absorbing piety of an unprecedented secular kind. The *New England Primer* had switched the letter "W" from "Whale" to "Washington": "By Washington/ Great deeds are done." A basic book on child development urged parents to heed Mirabeau's precept: "Begin with the infant in his cradle: let the first word he lisps be the name of WASHINGTON."[76] As though the press were doing penance for past trespasses, Americans published more than four hundred eulogies upon his death.

Despite lapses in self-discipline, he succeeded in sustaining the image of a demigod president proper to a democratic republic. He helped preserve that image for posterity. When his reports from the frontier were published as a pamphlet in 1754, he apologized for their imperfections as the result of having no time to "correct or amend the Diction." But a letter told his brother not to believe reports of his death and last words: "I take this early oppertunity of contradicting both." Sometime between 1781 and 1784, he amended that line to read, "I take this early opportunity of contradicting the first, and of assuring you, that I have not as yet composed the latter."[77]

For posterity, he elevated private letters to the more proper level of official correspondence composed by aides and secretaries. Joseph Reed, his first military secretary, said that General Washington lacked confidence in composition, sometimes adopting drafts inferior to his own "from an extreme diffidence in himself." Another aide, Timothy Pickering, agreed: "Whatever was destined to meet the public eye, he seems to have been fearful to exhibit." The general's style in private letters, he added, was adapted to the addressees, "perfectly plain and didactic," though sometimes inconsistent and incorrect.[78]

Later editors feared that these weaknesses demeaned the image Washington had forged for the future. His first editor, Jared Sparks, changed such lively descriptions as that of money being "but a flea-bite at present," to such formal locutions as "totally inadequate to our demands at present."[79] Belle Greene, J.P. Morgan's aide, refused to pass on to posterity Washington's "vulgar outpourings" and destroyed some of them.[80]

But thanks to Washington's meticulous habits, posterity would not be denied. His practice was to make multiple copies of documents—original, addressee's copy, duplicate in case of loss, a file copy, and another for government files.

He kept earlier drafts as well. These drafts enable us to see how, like the ancient giant Antaeus who stayed alive so long as he kept one foot on the ground, Washington privately suffered folly, frustration, and fallibility while publicly projecting the high moral purpose, high seriousness, and high style revered today.

NOTE ON THE TEXT

This story about George Washington's life in his own words relies on manuscripts at the Library of Congress. Earlier drafts are preferred as revealing consistency in a career based on "a steady and rigid attention to the rules of propriety." Explanatory notes or commentary on the context of Washington's words are included in parentheses or as headnotes. Bracketed and italicized text are quoted from eyewitnesses or interviews. Preparation of this material has been encouraged immeasurably by friends George Bilias, M.J. Francis, Charles Royster, and Dorothy Twohig.

1

GROWING UP VIRGINIAN

1738–1752

A fourth-generation American, George Washington was not born a gentleman. His great-grandfather, grandfather, and father had all been planters along the Potomac with more land than money, more family than noble ancestry. In the years of his celebrity he had to rely on sister Betty Lewis for genealogy, which was among the least of his concerns.

[Genealogy] is a subject to which I confess I have paid very little attention.... Very few cases, I believe, occur where a recurrence to pedigree for any considerable distance back has been found necessary to establish such points as may frequently arise in older Countries.[1]

My father Augustine married Jane Butler by whom he had my half-brothers Lawrence and Augustine. He then married Mary Ball with whom he had George, Betty, Samuel, John Augustine, Charles, and Mildred. My father died when I was only 10 years old.[2] He departed this life 1743, aged 49 years.[3]

Father Augustine, widowed at thirty-five, had then wed twenty-three-year-old Mary Ball of a London attorney's family, who, orphaned at twelve, added her substantial

---

property to his four thousand acres along the Potomac that included what would become Mount Vernon. She was twenty-four when George Washington was born in their four-room farmhouse at Pope's Creek, Westmoreland County, Virginia.

When he was six, they moved to their farm near Fredericksburg, closer to schooling. Neighbors would pool resources to hire a traveling tutor who taught chiefly by having pupils copy exercises from his notebooks into their own. Washington preserved his copies in folio-sized notebooks. Among them is a complete list of rules a young person would have to follow to behave like a gentleman, "Rules of Civility & Decent Behaviour in Company and Conversation." The 110 rules stressed self-control for propriety that would win friends and influence people. At age thirteen Washington struggled to copy all of them, as sampled below.

1st   Every Action done in Company, ought to be with some Sign of Respect to those that are Present.

2d   When in Company, put not your Hands to any Part of the Body, not usualy Discovered.

5th   If you Cough, Sneeze, Sigh, or Yawn, do it not Loud but Privately; and Speak not in your Yawning, but put Your handkercheif or Hand before your face and turn aside.

6th   Sleep not when others Speak, Sit not when others stand, Speak not when you Should hold your Peace, walk not on when others stop.

7th   Put not off your Cloths in the presence of Others, nor go out of your Chamber half Drest

8th   ——At Play and at Fire its Good manners to Give Place to the last Commer, and affect not to Speak Louder than Ordinary

9th Spit not in the Fire, nor stoop low before it neither Put your Hands into the Flames to warm them, nor Set your Feet upon the Fire especially if there be meat [food] before it

19th let your Countenance be pleasant but in Serious Matters Somewhat grave.

20th The Gestures of the Body must be Suited to the discourse you are upon.

24th Do not laugh too loud or too much at any Publick Spectacle.

25th Superfluous Complements and all Affectation of Ceremonie are to be avoided, yet where due they are not to be Neglected. . . .

> These rules of courtesy had been methodized by French Jesuits around 1600 and translated into English fifty years later. The rules stressed manners that were appropriate to one's station in the stratified cultures of France or Britain. As the younger son of an American colonial (in itself a mark of inferior culture), with little expectation of rising, the exercise in penmanship gave Washington a guide for behaving in highest society.

26th In Pulling off your Hat to Persons of Distinction, as Noblemen, Justices, Churchmen etc make a Reverence, bowing more or less according to the Custom of the Better Bred, and Quality of the Person. Amongst your equals expect not always that they Should begin with you first, but to Pull off the Hat when there is no need is Affectation, in the Manner of Saluting and resaluting in words keep to the most usual Custom.

27th Tis ill manners to bid one more eminent than yourself be covered as well as not to do it to whom it's due Likewise he that makes too much haste to Put on his hat does not well, yet he ought to Put it on at the first, or at most the Second time of being ask'd; now what is herein Spoken, of Qualification in behaviour in Saluting, ought also to be observed in taking of Place, and Sitting down for ceremonies without Bounds is troublesome

28th   If any one come to Speak to you while you are Sitting Stand up tho he be your Inferiour, and when you Present Seats let it be to every one according to his Degree [social status]

29th   When you meet with one of Greater Quality than yourself, Stop, and retire especially if it be at a Door or any Straight place to give way for him to Pass

30th   In walking the highest Place in most Countrys Seems to be on the right hand therefore Place yourself on the left of whom you desire to Honour: but if three walk together the mid Place is the most Honourable the wall is usually given to the most worthy if two walk together

33d   They that are in Dignity or in office have in all places Preceedency but whilst they are Young they ought to respect those that are their equals in Birth or other Qualitys, though they have no Publick charge.

36th——Artificers and Persons of low Degree ought not to use many ceremonies to Lords, or Others of high Degree but Respect and highly Honour them, and those of high Degree ought to treat them with affibility and Courtesie, without Arrogancy

37th——In Speaking to men of Quality do not lean nor Look them full in the Face, nor approach too near them at lest Keep a full Pace from them

42d   Let thy ceremonies in Courtesie be proper to the Dignity of his place with whom thou conversest for it is absurd to act the same with a Clown and a Prince

56th   Associate yourself with Men of good Quality if you Esteem your own Reputation; for 'tis better to be alone than in bad Company.

58th Let your Conversation be without Malice or Envy, for 'tis a Sign of a Tractable and Commendable Nature: And in all Causes of Passion admit Reason to Govern.
83d When you deliver a matter do it without Passion and with Discretion, however mean the Person be you do it too
105th Be not Angry at Table whatever happens and if you have reason to be so, Shew it not but on a Chearfull Countenance especially if there be Strangers for Good Humour makes one Dish of Meat a Feast
109th——Let your Recreations be Manfull not Sinfull.
110th——Labour to keep alive in your Breast that Little Spark of Celestial fire Called Conscience.[4]

At age sixteen, after his mother had vetoed his plans for a naval career, Washington turned to surveying not so much as a profession but as needed to establish property lines. His father had left him a little property along with surveying tools for that purpose. He learned the necessary plane geometry, and in spring 1748 he went along as an observer while taking notes on a survey team working in the trackless forests of the Shenandoah Valley. The team must have been as amused at naive Washington as he was in encountering the local nightlife.

Tuesday March 15th. We got our Suppers and was Lighted in to a Room and I not being so good a Woodsman as the rest of my Company striped my self very orderly and went in to the Bed as they call'd it when to my Surprize I found it to be nothing but a Little Straw—Matted together without Sheets or any thing else but only one Thread Bear blanket with double its Weight of Vermin such as Lice Fleas etc. I was glad to get up (as soon as the Light was carried from us) and put on my Cloths and Lay as my Companions. Had we not have been very tired, I am sure we should not have slep'd much that night. I made a Promise not to Sleep so from that time forward chusing rather to sleep in the open Air. . . .

Wednesday 16th. We set out early and finish'd about one oClock and then Travell'd up to Frederick Town where our Baggage came to us. We cleaned ourselves (to get Rid of the Game we had catched the Night before) and took a Review of the Town and then return'd to our Lodgings where we had a good Dinner prepar'd for us Wine and Rum Punch in Plenty and a good Feather Bed with clean Sheets which was a very agreable regale.

Thursday 17th. Rain'd till Ten oClock and then clearing we reached as far as Major [Andrew] Campbells one of there Burgesses about 25 Miles from Town. Nothing Remarkable this day nor Night but that we had a Tolerable good bed [to] lay on.

> The expedition also gave him a chance to record amused but not arrogant impressions of American Indian culture; a foreshadowing of adventures soon to follow.

Wednesday 23d. Rain'd till about two oClock and Clear'd when we were agreeably surpris'd at the sight of thirty odd Indians coming from War with only one Scalp. We had some Liquor with us of which we gave them Part it elevating there Spirits put them in the Humour of Dauncing of whom we had a War Daunce. There Manner of Dauncing is as follows Viz. They clear a Large Circle and make a great Fire in the Middle then seat themselves around it the Speaker makes a grand Speech telling them in what Manner they are to Daunce after he has finish'd the best Dauncer Jumps up as one awaked out of a Sleep and Runs and Jumps about the Ring in a most comicle Manner he is followd by the Rest then begins there Musicians to Play the Musick is a Pot half of Water with a Deerskin Streched over it as tight as it can and a goard with some Shott in it to Rattle and a Piece of an horses Tail tied to it to make it look fine the one keeps Rattling and the other Drumming all the While the others is Dauncing.

> Penetrating westward, the survey team came across German immigrant settlers; the van of their countrymen beginning to populate backwoods Pennsylvania. Washington's ill-tempered attitude seems prophetic. The immigrants harassed the team because a survey would result in their eviction as squatters—another foreshadowing, since the next generation of squatters would irritate Washington when he himself owned large tracts of underpopulated western lands.

Monday 4th. We did two Lots and was attended by a great Company of People Men Women and Children that attended us through the Woods as we went shewing there Antick tricks. I really think they seem to be as Ignorant a Set of People as the Indians. They would never speak English but when spoken to they speak all Dutch. This day our Tent was blown down by the Violentness of the Wind.

Wednesday the 13th. of April 1748. Mr. Fairfax got safe home and I myself safe to my Brothers which concludes my Journal.[5]

> By this time, Washington was living at Mount Vernon with his half-brother Lawrence, who was fourteen years older and who was a substitute father. As a Virginia marine, Lawrence had survived a disastrous expedition against the Spanish at Cartegena under Admiral Edward Vernon, after whom he named the family plantation. As a colonial with no hope for advancement, Lawrence returned home, volunteering as Adjutant General of Virginia in the spirit of noblesse oblige. He married into a neighboring family,

the Fairfaxes, who owned much of the Northern Neck; a connection that lifted him into the upper strata of Virginia society. Thus, at seventeen, George Washington had enough influence to be named Surveyor of Culpeper County, a job that took him back to the wilderness. Abandoning the luxury of the Fairfax mansion, Belvoir, for the brutal forest made him chafe at his fate.

———Amongst a parcel of Barbarian's and an uncooth set of People ... I seem to be in a Place where no real satisfaction be had. ... I have not sleep'd above three Nights or four in a bed but after Walking a good deal all the Day lay down before the fire upon a Little Hay Straw Fodder or bearskin which ever is to be had with Man Wife and Children like a Parcel of Dogs or Catts and happy's he that gets the Birth nearest the fire there's nothing would make it pass of tolerably but a good Reward and Doubbloon is my constant gain every Day that the Weather will permit my going out and sometime Six Pistoles the coldness of the Weather will not allow my making a long stay as the Lodging is rather too cold for the time of Year I have never had my Cloths of but lay and sleep in them like a Negro except the few Nights I have lay'n in Frederick Town.[6]

In sharp contrast, the Fairfax family must have provided finishing schooling. The ladies of the house, along with those of Fredericksburg, would have tutored him in social graces far beyond the "Rules of Civility." Typical Virginians, they would have danced till dawn or until the fiddler faltered, introducing Washington to a lifetime passion for dancing. Their play readings in the parlor would have inspired a passion for theatricals, especially Joseph Addison's *Cato*, about the noble Roman patriot who preferred death to dishonor—which Washington could quote by heart and his soldiers would perform for him many years later. The ladies even had him at seventeen copying romantic verse from *The Gentleman's Magazine* and composing laments for unrequited love to lowland beauty Betsy Fauntleroy.

My Place of Residence is at present at his Lordships [Belvoir] where I might was my heart disengag'd pass my time very pleasantly as theres a very agreeable Young Lady Lives in the same house (Colo. George Fairfax's Wife's sister) but as thats only adding Fuel to fire it makes me the more uneasy for by often and unavoidably being in Company with her revives my former Passion for your Low Land Beauty whereas was I to live more retired from young Women I might in some measure eleviate my sorrows by burying that chaste and troublesome Passion in the grave of oblivion or eternall forgetfulness for as I am very well assured that's the only antidote or remedy that I ever shall be releivd by or only recess than can administer any cure or help to me as I am well convinced was I ever to attempt any thing I should only get a denial which would be only adding grief to uneasiness.[7]

> At nineteen, Washington finally sailed the ocean when he accompanied his brother Lawrence to Barbados. Lawrence had long suffered some kind of lung disease and in the fall of 1751 he sought comfort in a milder climate. As now habitual with him, George Washington kept a journal not of introspection but of records of people, places, and events such as their harrowing voyage during hurricane season or his catching smallpox—which left his face pitted but gave him lifetime immunity.

October 20th, 1751. A Constant succession of hard Winds, Squals of Rain, and Calms was the remarkable attendants of this day which was so sudden and flighty we durst not go under any but reef'd Sails and those that we cou'd double reef. At 6 AM put about to the Eastward. A sloop that for the two preceding Days was in sight of us hung out a Signal but whether distress or not we are uncertain; if it had were incapable of relieving them by the contrariness of the winds.

October 30th. This Morning arose with agreeably assurances of a certain and steady trade Wind which after near five Weeks buffiting and being toss'd by a fickle and Merciless ocean was glad'ening knews.

November 2d. We were greatly alarm'd with the cry of Land at 4 AM we quitted our beds with surprise and found the land plainly appearing at bout 3 leauges distance when by our reckonings we shou'd have been near 150 Leagues to the Windward we to Leeward about the distance above mention'd and had we been but 3 or 4 leauges more we shou'd have been out of sight of the Island run down the Latitude and probably not have discover'd Error in time to have gain'd land for 3 Weeks or More

4th. This morning received a card from Major Clarke, welcoming us to Barbadoes, with an invitation to breakfast and dine with him. We went—myself with some reluctance, as the smallpox was in his family.

5th. Early this morning came Dr. Hilary, an eminent physician recommended by Major Clarke, to pass his opinion on my brother's disorder, which he did in a favorable light, giving great assurances, that it was not so fixed but that a cure might be effectually made. In the cool of the evening we rode out accompanied by Mr. Carter to seek lodgings in the country, as the Doctor advised, and was perfectly ravished by the beautiful prospects which on every side presented to our view The fields of Cain, Corn, Fruit Trees, etc in a delightful Green. We return'd without accomplishing our intentions.

Saturday 17th. Was strongly attacked with the small Pox: Sent for Dr. Lanahan whose attendance was very constant till my recovery, and going out which was not 'till thursday the 12th of December.

Still seeking a cure, Lawrence sailed on to Bermuda leaving his brother to return home alone. George Washington reached Mount Vernon in March 1751 after a voyage that gave him time to review but not reflect on what he had seen; particularly government, agriculture, and high society different from that at Belvoir.

Sunday 22d. The Governor of Barbados seems to keep a proper State: Lives very retired and at Little expence it is said he is a Gentleman of good sence. As he avoids the Errors of his predecessors he gives no handle for complaint but at the same time by declining much familiarity is not over zealously beloved. . . .

The Earth in most parts is extremely rich and as black as our richest Marsh. . . . One-third of their Land or nearly genearily is in Canes for Harvest the rest is in young Cane guinea Corn (which greatly supports their Negros) Yams plantens Potatos and ginger and some small part left waste for Stock. Their dung they are very careful in saving, and curious in making which they do by throwing up large heaps of Earth and a number of Stakes drove therein Sufficient for Sixteen head of Cattle to Stand seperately tied too which they are three months together trampling all the trash etc and then its fit to manure the Ground. Provisions in General are very indeferent but much better than the same quantity of pasturage wou'd afford in Virginia. The very grass that grows amongst their corn is not Lost but carefully gather'd for provender for their Stock.

Hospitality and a Genteel behavior is shewn to every gentlemen stranger by the Gentlemen Inhabitants . . . The

Ladys Generally are very agreeable but by ill custom affect the Negro Style. . . . There are few who may be calld middling people they are either very rich or very poor for by a Law of the Island Every Gentleman is oblig'd to keep a white person for ten Acres capable of acting in the Militia and consequently those persons so kept cant but [be] very poor.

In the midst of such analytical observations, Washington amused himself in the privacy of his journal by reporting on the consequences of unbridled passion.

January 23d. This day enticed the Mate to come from his Cabbin (as a snail enlivened by the genial heat of the Sun) who has since the third or fourth day after leaving Barbados been coop'd up with a fashionable disorder contracted there.

2

CONFRONTING HUMAN NATURE IN THE WILD

OCTOBER 1753–JANUARY 1754

Lawrence Washington returned from Bermuda the next year to die (26 July 1752), leaving Mount Vernon to his wife and daughter. They leased it to George Washington. Governor Robert Dinwiddie gave him Lawrence's post as Adjutant General of militia. The post had become limited to the Southern District, but by 1754 he was granted the Northern Neck with rank of major. With no prior military experience, but knowing the frontier from earlier surveys, he volunteered to carry the Governor's eviction notice to French soldiers squatting on British lands.

A half-dozen years earlier, a syndicate that included George Washington's half-brothers and Governor Dinwiddie formed the Ohio Company. The company was entitled to five hundred thousand acres in the Ohio Valley if they could settle the land. They had already built a road from Wills Creek, Maryland, to the Monongahela River, but to block their progress, Canada's Governor Duquesne had been building a chain of forts including Fort Presque Isle (Erie, Pennsylvania) and Fort Le Boeuf

(Waterford, Pennsylvania) toward which Washington headed.[1] If Belvoir served as a finishing school for social graces, the wilderness offered advanced training in duplicity.

Washington set out on 31 October 1753, picking up a team of experienced frontiersmen along with a messenger to carry reports back to the Governor, who subsequently published them.

At a most inclement Season, for [Washington] travelled over the Apalachean Mountains, and passed 250 Miles thro an uninhabited wilderness country (except by a few tribes of Indians settled on the Banks of the Ohio) to Presque Isle within 15 miles of Lake Erie in the depth of the winter when the whole face of the Earth was covered with snow and the waters covered with Ice;—The whole distance from Williamsburg the then seat of Government at least 500 miles. It was on this occasion he was named by the half-King (as he was called) and the tribes of Nations with whom he treated—Caunotaucarius (in English) the Towntaker.[2]

The Indians called him the name first given to his great grandfather, John Washington. Now contemporary reports to the Governor provided a vivid sense of young Washington's frustration in the tug of war with the French over the allegiance of his Indian friends.

October 25th, 1753. About 3 o'Clock this Evening the Half-King came to [Logs]Town; I went up and invited him and [interpreter John] Davison, privately, to my Tent, and desir'd him to relate some of the Particulars of his Journey to the French Commandant, and Reception there; and so give me an Account of the Ways and Distance. He told me, that the nearest and levellest Way was now impassable, by Reason of many large miry Savannas; that we must be obliged to go by Venango, and should not get to the near Fort under 5 or 6 Night's Sleep, good Travelling. . . .

26th. As I had Orders to make all possible Dispatch, and waiting here was very contrary to my Inclination, I thanked [the Half-King] in the most suitable Manner I could, and told him that my Business required the greatest Expedition, and would not admit of Delay. He was not well pleased that I should offer to go before the Time he had appointed, and told me that he could not consent to our going without a Guard, for Fear some Accident should befal us, and draw a Reflection upon him; and accordingly he gave Orders to . . . two Men of their Nation to be in readiness to set out with us next Morning. As I found it was impossible to get off without affronting them in the most egregious Manner, I consented to stay. . . .

29th. The Half-King and Monocatoocha, came very early, and begged me to stay one Day more, for notwithstanding they had used all Diligence in their Power, the Shanoah Chiefs had not brought the Wampum they ordered, but would certainly be in To-night; if not, they would delay me no longer, but would send it after us as soon as they arrived: When I found them so pressing in their Request, and knew that returning of Wampum [to the French] was the abolishing of Agreements and giving this up, was shaking of all Dependence upon the French, I consented to stay, as I believed an Offence offered at this Crisis, might be attended with greater ill Consequence, than another Day's Delay. They also informed me that Shingiss could not get in his Men, and was prevented from coming himself by his Wife's Sickness, (I believe, by Fear of the French).

Upon reaching their camp at Venango, Washington confronted more seasoned French officers. Trying to wean the Indians from his side, they gained more time by obstructing delivery of the Governor's message. Washington's suspicions of both the Indians and the French turned to anxiety.

4th [December]. We found the French Colours hoisted at a House which they drove Mr. John Frazier, an English Subject, from; I immediately repaired to it, to know where the Commander resided: There were three Officers, one of whom, Capt. [Philippe] Joncaire, inform'd me, that he had the Command of the Ohio, but that there was a General Officer at the near Fort, which he advis'd me to for an Answer. He invited us to sup with them, and treated us with the greatest Complaisance.

The Wine, as they dosed themselves pretty plentifully with it, soon banished the Restraint which at first appear'd in their Conversation, and gave a License to their Tongues to reveal their Sentiments more freely.

They told me, That it was their absolute Design to take Possession of the Ohio, and by G—they would do it; for that they were sensible the English could raise two Men for their one; yet they knew, their Motions were too slow and dilatory to prevent any Undertaking of theirs. They pretend to have an undoubted Right to the River, from a Discovery made by one La Sol 60 Years ago; and the Rise of this Expedition is, to prevent our settling on the River or Waters of it, as they have heard of some Families moving out in Order thereto. . . .

5th. Rain'd excessively all Day, which prevented our Travelling. Capt. Joncaire sent for the Half-King, as he had but just heard that he came with me: he affected to be much concern'd that I did not make free to bring them in before; I excused it in the best Manner I was capable, and told him I did not think their Company agreeable, as I had heard him say a good deal in Dispraise of Indians in general; but another Motive prevented me from bringing them into his

Company; I knew he was Interpreter, and a Person of very great Influence among the Indians, and had lately used all possible Means to draw them over to their Interest; therefore I was desirous of giving no Opportunity that could be avoided.

When they came in, there was great Pleasure express'd at seeing them; he wonder'd how they could be so near without coming to visit him, made several trifling Presents, and applied Liquor so fast, that they were soon render'd incapable of the Business they came about, nowithstanding the Caution that was given.

6th. The Half-King came to my Tent, quite sober, and insisted very much that I should stay and hear what he had to say to the French; I fain would have prevented his speaking any Thing, 'til he came to the Commandant; but could not prevail: He told me, that at this Place a Council Fire was kindled, where all their Business with these People was to be transacted, and that the Management of the Indian Affairs was left solely to Monsieur Joncaire. As I was desirous of knowing the Issue of this, I agreed to stay, but sent our Horses a little Way up French Creek, to raft over and encamp; which I knew would make it near Night.

7th. We found it extremely difficult getting the Indians off To-day, as every Stratagem had been used to prevent their going up with me: I had last Night left John Davison (the Indian Interpreter that I brought from the Loggs-Town with me) strictly charg'd not to be out of their Company, as I could not get them over to my Tent . . . but was obliged to send Mr.[Christopher] Gist over To-day to fetch them, which he did with great Persuasion.

At 11 o'Clock we set out for the Fort; and were prevented from arriving there 'til the 11th by excessive Rains, Snows, and bad Travelling, through many Mires and

Swamps, which we were obliged to pass, to avoid crossing the Creek, which was impossible, either by fording or rafting, the Water was so high and rapid.

12th. I prepar'd early to wait upon the Commander [Legardeur de St. Pierre], and was received and conducted to him by the second Officer in Command; I acquainted him with my Business, and offer'd my Commission and Letter, both of which he desired me to keep 'til the Arrival of Monsieur Riparti [Sieur de Repentigny], Captain, at the next Fort, who was sent for and expected every Hour. . . .

At 2 o'Clock the Gentleman that was sent for arrived, when I offer'd the Letter, etc. again; which they receiv'd, and adjourn'd into a private Apartment for the Captain to translate, who understood a little English; after he had done it, the Commander desired I would walk in, and bring my Interpreter to peruse and correct it; which I did.

14th. This Evening I received an Answer to his Honour the Governor's Letter from the Commandant.

> The commandant rejected the letter, insisting that it should have been addressed to Governor Duquesne in Canada. He also disputed the Americans' claim that the French were trespassing.

15th. The Commandant ordered a plentiful Store of Liquor, Provision, etc. to be put on Board our Canoe, and appeared to be extremely complaisant, though he was exerting every Artifice that he could invent to set our own Indians at Variance with us, to prevent their going 'til after our Departure: Presents, Rewards, and every Thing that could be suggested by him or his Officers.

I can't say that ever in my Life I suffer'd so much Anxiety as I did in this Affair; I saw that every Stratagem that the most fruitful Brain could invent, was practised, to win the Half-King to their Interest, and that leaving Him here was giving them the Opportunity they aimed at.

I went to the Half-King, and press'd him in the strongest Terms to go: He told me the Commandant would not discharge him 'til the Morning. I then went to the Commandant, and desired him to do their Business, and complain'd of ill Treatment; for keeping them, as they were Part of my Company, was detaining me; which he promised not to do, but to forward my Journey as much as he could: He protested he did not keep them, but was ignorant of the Cause of their Stay; though I soon found it out:— He had promised them a Present of Guns, etc. if they would wait 'til the Morning.

As I was very much press'd, by the Indians, to wait this Day for them, I consented, on a Promise, That nothing should hinder them in the Morning.

16th. The French were not slack in their Inventions to keep the Indians this Day also; but as they were obligated, according to Promise, to give the Present, they then endeavoured to try the Power of Liquor, which I doubt not would have prevailed at any other Time than this, but I urged and insisted with the King so closely upon his Word, that he refrained, and set off with us as he had engaged.

Washington still faced conflict with both man and nature in the raw.

We had a tedious and very fatiguing Passage down the Creek, several Times we had like to have been staved against Rocks, and many Times were obliged all Hands to get out and remain in the Water Half an Hour or more, getting over the Shoals; at one Place the Ice had lodged and made it impassable by Water; therefore we were obliged to carry our Canoe across a Neck of Land, a Quarter of a Mile over.

We did not reach Venango, till the 22d, where we met with our Horses.[3]

23rd. Our Horses were now so weak and feeble, and the Baggage heavy, as we were obliged to provide all the Necessaries that the Journey would require; that we doubted much their performing it: therefore myself and others (except the Drivers which were obliged to ride) gave up our Horses for Packs, to assist along with the Baggage. I put myself in an Indian walking Dress, and continued with them three Days, till I found there was no Probability of their getting in, in any reasonable Time; the Horses grew less able to travel every Day; the Cold increased very fast, and the Roads were becoming much worse by a deep Snow, continually freezing; and as I was uneasy to get back, to make report of my Proceedings to his Honour the Governor, I determined to prosecute my Journey the nearest Way through the Woods, on Foot.

I took my necessary Papers, pulled off my Cloaths; tied myself up in a Match Coat; and with my Pack at my Back with my Papers and Provisions in it, and a Gun, set out with Mr. Gist, fitted in the same Manner, on Wednesday the 26th.

The Day following, just after we had left a place called the Murdering-Town, where we intended to quit the Path, and steer across the Country for Shannapins Town, we fell in with a Party of French Indians, who had lain in Wait for us; one of them fired at Mr. Gist or me, not 15 Steps, but fortunately missed.

Gist's journal adds more vivid details of their peril.

[Got to the Murthering town, on the southeast fork of Beaver creek. Here we met with an Indian, whom I thought I had seen at Joncaire's, at Venango. Major Washington insisted

on travelling on the nearest way to the forks of Alleghany. We asked the Indian if he could go with us, and show us the nearest way. We travelled very brisk for 8 or 10 miles, when the Major's feet grew very sore, and he very weary, and the Indian steered too much north-eastwardly. The Major desired to encamp, to which the Indian asked to carry his gun. But he refused that, and then the Indian grew churlish. I thought very ill of the fellow, but did not care to let the Major know I mistrusted him. But he soon mistrusted him as much as I. Before we came to water, we came to a clear meadow; it was very light, and snow on the ground. The Indian made a stop, turned about; the Major saw him point his gun toward us and fire. Said the Major, "Are you shot?"

"No," said I. Upon which the Indian ran to a big standing white oak, and to loading his gun; but we were soon with him. I would have killed him; but the Major would not suffer me to kill him.

I said to the Major, "As you will not have him killed, we must get him away, and then we must travel all night."[4]]

We took this Fellow into Custody, and kept him till about 9 o'Clock at Night, and then let him go, and walked all the remaining Part of the Night without making any Stop, that we might get the Start, so far, as to be out of the Reach of their Pursuit the next Day, as we were well assured they would follow our Tract as soon as it was light: The next Day we continued travelling till quite dark, and got to the River about two Miles above Shannapins; we expected to have found the River frozen, but it was not, only about 50 Yards from each Shore; the Ice I suppose had broke up above, for it was driving in vast Quantities.

There was no Way for getting over but on a Raft, which we set about, with but one poor Hatchet, and got finished just after Sun-setting, after a whole Days Work; we got it launched, and on Board of it, and set off; but before we were Half Way over, we were jammed in the Ice in such a Manner that we expected every Moment our Raft to sink, and ourselves to perish; I put out my setting Pole to try to stop the Raft, that the Ice might pass by, when the Rapidity of the Stream threw it with so much Violence against the Pole, that it jirked me out into ten Feet Water, but I fortunately saved myself by catching hold of one of the Raft logs; notwithstanding all our Efforts we could not get the Raft to either Shore, but were obliged, as we were near an Island, to quit our Raft and make to it.

The Cold was so extremely severe, that Mr. Gist, had all his Fingers, and some of his Toes frozen, and the Water was shut up so hard, that we found no Difficulty in getting off the Island, on the Ice, in the Morning, and went to Mr. Frazier's. . . .

Despite exhaustion from confronting both enemy and environment, Washington remained mindful of courtesy, amusing himself with a visit to a venerable friend.

I went up about three Miles to the Mouth of Yaughyaughgane to visit Queen Alliquippa, who had expressed great Concern that we passed her in going to the Fort. I made her a Present of a Matchcoat and a Bottle of Rum, which latter was thought much the best Present of the two.[5]

Heading home, he met a group on their way to the upper Ohio Valley territory he had just left. They proposed to build a fort, now Pittsburgh, that would protect English settlement on the western frontier from French forces numbering fifteen hundred and growing. To protect the fort, Governor Dinwiddie responded with a military force the next spring. He promoted George Washington to Lieutenant Colonel and second in command of an expedition bound for disaster.

3

FINDING FAME
ON THE FRONTIER

MAY 1754–DECEMBER 1758

Before Lieutenant Colonel Washington could reach the
half-built fort at the Monongahela it had fallen to the
French. By that time, the death of Colonel Joshua Fry had
left him in command. As he approached Great Meadow,
Indian allies warned him of French patrols nearby. Realiz-
ing his innocence in guerrilla tactics, Washington again
relied on old friends Christopher Gist and the Half King.
Still, he had developed subtle tactics of his own, such as
recruiting young Indian allies.

May 27. I did not fail to let the young Indians who were
in our Camp know, that the French wanted to kill the Half
King; and that had its desired effect. They thereupon offered to accompany our People to go after the French. . . .
About eight at Night, received an Express from the Half
King, which informed me, that, as he was coming to join
us, he had seen along the Road the Tracks of two Men, which
he had followed, till he was brought thereby to a low ob-
scure Place that he was of Opinion the whole Party of the
French was hidden there.

Experience gained several months earlier had taught him to be more circumspect in guerrilla fighting.

That very Moment I sent out Forty Men, and ordered my Ammunition to be put in a Place of Safety, under a strong Guard to defend it, fearing it to be a Stratagem of the French to attack our Camp; and with the rest of my Men, set out in a heavy Rain, and in a Night as dark as Pitch, along a Path scarce broad enough for one Man; we were sometimes fifteen or twenty Minutes out of the Path, before we could come to it again, and so dark, that we would often strike one against another.

All Night long we continued our Rout, and the 28th, about Sun-rise, we arrived at the Indian Camp, where, after having held a Council with the Half King, it was concluded we should fall on them together . . . marching one after the other, in the Indian Manner. We were advanced pretty near to them, as we thought, when they discovered us; whereupon I ordered my Company to fire; mine was supported by [Lieutenant Thomas Waggoner's] and my Company and his received the whole Fire of the French, during the greatest Part of the Action, which only lasted a Quarter of an Hour, before the Enemy was routed.

We killed Mr. de Jumonville, the Commander of the Party, as also nine others; we wounded one, and made Twenty-one Prisoners . . . The Indians scalped the Dead, and took away the most part of their Arms, after which we marched on with the Prisoners and the Guard to the Indian Camp.[1]

The *Pennsylvania Gazette*, 27 June 1754, reported that as the French tried to retreat, the Indians ambushed them, scalping five before Washington interfered. The Half King insisted on scalping them all, alleging, "Those People had killed, boiled, and eat his Father," but Washington persuaded him five scalps were sufficient. One of those five was Jumonville, the commander, "whom the Half King himself dispatched with his tomahawk."

The official French version, however, would say that Washington's men had killed Jumonville with a musket ball through the head and would have killed all the rest if the Indians had not stopped them.[2] Worse, they claimed Jumonville was an unarmed diplomat killed while trying to negotiate peace. They used Washington's own intercepted reports as evidence of his romantic impetuosity.

May 31. We expect every Hour to be attacked by a superior Force, but shall if they stay one day longer be prepared for them; We have already got Intrenchments and are about a Pallisado'd Fort, which will I hope be finished today. . . . I fortunately escaped without a wound, tho' the right Wing where I stood was exposed to and received all the Enemy's fire and was the part where the man was killed and the rest wounded. I can with truth assure you, I heard the Bullets whistle and believe me there was something charming in the sound.[3]

Critics in London called that remark the ravings of a "brave braggart,"[4] while the King himself groused, "He would not say so, if he had been used to hear many."[5]

About 9 Oclock on the 3d of July the Enemy advanced with Shouts, & dismal Indian yells to our Intrenchments. . . . They then, from every little rising—tree—stump— Stone—and bush kept up a constant galding fire upon us; which was returned in the best manner we could till late in the afternoon when their fell the most tremendous rain that can be conceived—filled our trenches with Water—Wet, not only the Ammunition in the Cartouch boxes and firelocks, but that which was in a small temporary Stock-

ade in the middle of the Intrenchment called Fort Necessity erected for the sole purpose of its security, and that of
the few stores we had; and left us nothing but a few (for all
were not provided with them) Bayonets for defence.

In this situation and no [prospect] of bettering it terms
of capitulation were offered to us by the [enemy] which
with some alterations that were insisted upon were the more
readily acceded to, as we had no Salt provisions, and but
indifferently supplied with fresh; which, from the heat of
the Weather, would not keep; and because a full third of
our Numbers Officers as well as privates were, by this time,
killed or wounded—The next morning we marched out
with the honors of War. . . . [6]

> The Half King ridiculed both sides as fools, especially
> Washington, who—though good-natured but lacking
> experience—treated the Indians as slaves, and would never
> listen to them but insisted on their fighting a coward's way.[7]
>
> Captured at the hastily built Fort Necessity, unable to
> read French, Washington unwittingly confessed in the
> Articles of Capitulation to having "assassinated"
> Jumonville.
>
> The French published his confession along with his
> diary and other papers as proof of British warlike aims on
> the Pennsylvania frontier—a pretext for the French and
> Indian War that followed. At the same time, London
> critics reviled the confession as, "The most infamous a
> British Subject ever put his Hand to."[8] Washington's
> defense was that he had no alternative but to surrender
> and that he had been deceived by his interpreter's duplic-
> ity. Eyewitness Adam Stephen said Washington's translator
> had been forced to translate from spoken rather than
> written texts: "We could scarcely keep the Candle light to
> read them; they were wrote in a bad Hand, on wet and

blotted Paper. . . . There was no such Word as Assassination mentioned."⁹

After the campaign, the Governor responded by breaking the militia into independent companies. This meant demoting the twenty-three-year-old colonel to captain, ranking below officers with royal commissions. In October 1754, while protesting, "My inclinations are strongly bent to arms," Washington's sense of injured merit compelled him to resign.

I must be reduced to a very low Command, and subjected to that of many who have acted as my inferior Officers. In short, every Captain, bearing the King's Commission; every half-pay Officer, or other, appearing with such commission, would rank before me; for these reasons, I choose to submit to the loss of Health, which I have, however, sustained (not to mention that of Effects [i.e., fever and headache]) and the fatigue I have undergone in our first Efforts; than subject myself to the same inconveniences, and run the risque of a second disappointment. I shall have the consolation itself, of knowing, that I have opened the way when the smallness of our numbers exposed us to the attacks of a Superior Enemy; That I have hitherto stood the heat and brunt of the Day, and escaped untouched, in time of extreme danger; and that I have the Thanks of my Country, for the Services I have rendered it. . . . Ingenuous treatment, and plain dealing, I at least expected.¹⁰

Washington's troops protested on his behalf, attesting to his popularity and fame, but he left a soldier's life behind for a home at Mount Vernon. When Lawrence Washington's daughter died in 1754, her mother remarried and leased the plantation to George Washington. He aimed to settle down as a country squire. But when General Edward Braddock came to drive the French from the Ohio, he appealed to Washington's ego and expertise. Pride and inclination thus cut short a six-month sulk in retirement. Washington rationalized a return to arms.

I can very truely say I have no expectation of reward but the hope of meriting the love of my Country, and friendly regard of my acquaintances; and as to any prospect of attaining a Commission, I have none, as I am pretty well assur'd it is not in General Braddocks power to give such a one as I woud accept off; as I am told a Company is the highest Command that is invested in his gift. He desird my Company this Campaigne, has honour'd me with particular marks of Esteem, and kindly envited me into his Family [i.e., staff]; which will ease me of that expence, which otherwise, woud unavoidably have accrued in furnishing a proper Camp Provision; whereas the expence will now be easy, (comparitively speaking) as baggage Horses, Tents, and some other necessarys will constitute the whole of the charge.[11]

> Well aware that such explanations might be "construed into self-applause," he claimed to have been "importuned" by Braddock, "who I suppose, imagined the small knowledge I have of the Country, Indians, etc worthy his notice."[12]
>
> Braddock ordered massive baggage and artillery hauled through the wilderness in a line three or four miles long. When that bogged down, he asked Washington, who was suffering from severe fever, for advice. Just as the Half King had complained about him, so now Washington complained that Braddock ignored advice.

I urgd it in the warmest terms I was master off, to push on if we even did it with a chosen Detachment for that purpose, with the Artillery and such other things as were absolutely necessary; leaving the Baggage and other Convoys with the Remainder of the Army, to follow by slow and regular Marches, which they might do safely while we were advanced in Front. . . . [but] I found, that instead of pushing on with vigour, without regarding a little rough Road, they were halting to Level every Mold Hill, and to erect Bridges over every brook; by which means we were 4 Days getting 12 Miles.[13]

> After Braddock ordered him left behind because of illness, Washington recovered enough to play a samaritan's role in the Wills Creek massacre, which he would recall vividly in later years but at the time defused the horror with a wry remark to brother Jack that reports of his death had been exaggerated.

As I have heard since my arrival at this place [Fort Cumberland] a circumstantial account of my death and dying Speech, I take this early oppertunity of contradicting both, and of assuring you that I [remain one] of the living by the miraculous care of Providence that protected me beyond all human expectation; I had 4 Bullets through my Coat, and two Horses shot under and yet escaped unhurt.[14]

The 8th of July I rejoined (in a covered Waggon) the advanced division of the Army under the immediate Command of the General. On the 9th I attended him on horse back tho very weak and low—on this day he was attacked and defeated by a party of French & Indians adjudged not to exceed 300. . . . [15]

> Many years later, for would-be biographer David Humphreys, Washington would refer to himself as "G.W." in recounting the horror of the massacre.

The General received the Wound of which he died; but

previous to it, had several horses killed and disabled under him. Captains [Robert] Orme and [Roger] Morris his two Aids de Camp having received wounds which rendered them unable to attend, G.W. remained the sole aid throughout the day, to the General; he also had one horse killed, and two wounded under him—A ball through his hat—and several through his clothes, but escaped unhurt. . . .

No person knowing in the disordered State things were who the Surviving Senior Officer was and the Troops by degrees going off in confusion without a ray of hope left of further opposition from those that remained G.W. placed the General in a small covered Cart, which carried some of his most essential equipage, and in the best order he could, with the last Troops (who only continued to be fired at) brought him over the *first* ford of the Monongahela; where they were formed in the best order circumstances would admit on a piece of rising ground; after which, by the generals order, he rode forward to halt those which had been earlier in the Retreat.

Accordingly, after crossing the Monongahela the *second time* and ascending the heights . . . he delivered the Generals order and then returned to report the situation he found them in—When he was again requested by the General whom he met coming on, in his litter with the first halted troops, to proceed (it then being after sundown) to the second division under the command of Colonel Dunbar, to make arrangements for covering the retreat, and forwarding on provisions and refreshments to the retreating and wounded Soldiers—

The shocking Scenes which presented themselves in this Nights March are not to be described—The dead—the dying—the groans—lamentations—and crys along the Road of the wounded for help (for those under the latter descriptions endeavoured from the first commencement of the action—or rather confusion—to escape to the second division) were enough to pierce a heart of adamant, the gloom and horror of which was not a little encreased by the impervious darkness occasioned by the close shade of thick woods which in places rendered it impossible for the two guides which attended to know when they were in, or out of the track but by groping on the ground with their hands. . . .

As soon as the two divisions united, the whole retreated towards Fort Cumberland; and at an Incampment near the Great Meadows the brave, but unfortunate General Braddock breathed his last. He was interred with the honors of war, and as it was left to G.W. to see this performed, and to mark out the spot for the reception of his remains—to guard against a savage triumph, if the place should be discovered—they were deposited in the Road over which the Army, Waggons etc. passed to hide every trace by which the entombment could be discovered.[16]

> "Heroic youth" Washington was now celebrated in sermon as an example of martial spirit, "a sacred Heaven-born Fire."[17] He was not finished yet. With Virginia's frontier exposed to French and Indian raids, the governor again promoted him to colonel and placed Virginia's defenses entirely under Washington's command. With headquarters at Fort Cumberland, Maryland, he was technically outranked by a captain holding a royal commission. Sick, miserable over defeat, and angry at the high command's failure to reward his heroics, he was moved to resign once more. In August 1755 he reprised his career.

It is with some difficulty and fatigue that I visit my Plantations in the [Northern] Neck, so much has a sickness of five weeks continuance reduced me . . . I am so little dispirited at what has happened, that I am always ready, and always willing to do my Country any Services that I am capable of; but never upon the Terms I have done, having suffer'd much in my private fortune beside impairing one of the best of Constitution's.

I was employ'd to go a journey in the Winter (when I believe few or none woud have undertaken it) and what did I get by it? my expences borne! I then was appointed with trifling Pay to conduct an handfull of Men to the Ohio. What did I get by this? Why, after putting myself to a considerable expence in equipping and providing Necessarys for the Campaigne—I went out, was soundly beaten, lost them all—came in, and had my Command taken from me or in other words my Command reduced, under *pretence* of an Order from home. I then went out a Volunteer with General Braddock and lost all my Horses and many other things but this being a voluntary act I shoud not have mention'd it, was it not to shew that I have been upon the loosing order ever since I enterd the Service, which is now near two Year's.[18]

> Honor dictated that Washington go on. Spurred by increasing fame, he accepted command to defend the Shenandoah Valley—despite lack of able troops, adequate supplies, political support, or appropriate authority. Twice he appealed in person (dressed in his Virginia militia uniform) to the high command: in 1756 to General William Shirley at Boston, and the next year to his successor John Campbell, Lord Loudon, at Philadelphia, who had heard of him only as "simple and young."[19] Washington found petitions useless. Three years of intense fighting along 350 wilderness miles counted for nothing in the regular army's eyes. But surviving the Braddock disaster was only one of a series of

dispensations that would lead some persons to think of themselves as somehow blessed.

A circumstance occurred which involved the life of G.W. in as much jeopardy as it had ever been before or since. The enemy sent out a large detachment to reconnoitre our Camp, and to ascertain our strength; in consequence of Intelligence that they were within 2 Miles of the Camp a party commanded by Lt Col Mercer of the Virginia line (a gallant and good Officer) was sent to dislodge them between whom a Severe conflict and hot firing ensued which lasting some time and appearing to approach the Camp it was conceived that our party was yielding the ground upon which G.W. with permission of the General called (per dispatch) for Volunteers and immediately marched at their head to sustain, as was conjectured the retiring troops. Led on by the firing till he came within less than half a mile, and it ceasing, he detached Scouts to investigate the cause and to communicate his approach to his friend Col Mercer advancing slowly in the meantime.

But it being near dusk and the intelligence not having been fully dissiminated among Col Mercers Corps, and they taking us, for the enemy who had retreated approaching in another direction commenced a heavy fire upon the relieving party which drew fire in return in spite of all the exertions of the Officers one of whom and several privates were killed and many wounded before a stop could be put to it, to accomplish which G.W. never was in more imminent danger by being between two fires, knocking up with his sword the presented pieces.[20]

In [another] of his tours along the frontier posts—he narrowly escaped, according to the account afterwards given by some of our People who were Prisoners with them, and eyewitnesses at the time, falling by an Indian party who

34

had waylaid (for another purpose) the communication along which with a small party of horse only he was passing—the road in this place formed a curve—and the prey they were in weight for being expected at the reverse part, the Captain of the party had gone across to observe the number [and] manner of their movement etc. in order that he might make his disposition accordingly leaving orders for the party not to take notice of any passengers the other way till he returned to them—in the mean time in the opposite direction I passed and escaped almost certain destruction for the weather was raining and the few Carbines unfit for use if we had escaped the first fire.

> Thus blessed, Washington felt obligated to answer his colony's recall to arms only to be once again denied victory over the French foe.

An Expedition against Fort Du Quesne was concerted, and undertaken under the conduct of General [John] Forbes; who tho a brave and good Officer, was so much debilitated by bad health, and so illy supplied with the means to carry on the expedition, that it was November before the Troops got to Loyal hanning: 50 or 60 miles short of Du Quesne . . . the Brigade [with troops from four colonies] commanded by G.W. being the leading one. . . . When the Army had got within about 12 or 15 miles of the Fort the enemy dispairing of its defence, blew it up—having first embarked their Artillery Stores and Troops—and retreated by water down the Ohio to their Settlements below.

Thus ended the Campaign, a little before Christmas in very inclement weather; and the last one made during that War by G.W. whose health by this time (as it had been declining for many months before occasioned by an inveterate disorder in his Bowels) became so precarious as to induce him (having seen quiet restored by this event to the

Frontiers of his own Country which was the principle inducement to his taking arms) to resign his Military appointments.[21]

4

PLANTING REBELLION

JANUARY 1759–APRIL 1775

Washington's ill health was reason enough to retire from military life. His malaria and dysentery had turned so severe in March of 1758 that he left his command at Winchester for treatment in Williamsburg. Six months later he was composing a celebrated letter confessing love to his neighbor's fun-loving wife, Sally Fairfax (12 September 1758). At eighteen, a slender, tall brunette with sparkling dark eyes, she and her sisters exchanged teasing letters with Washington, apparently tutoring him in the art of courtly correspondence. The love letter could have been another exercise in courtly composition rather than the overflow of powerful feelings, since he carefully revised the expression.

I profess myself a Votary to Love—I acknowledge that a Lady is in the Case—and further I confess, that this Lady is known to you.—Yes Madam, as well as she is to one, who is too sensible of her Charms to deny the Power, whose Influence he feels and must ever Submit to. I feel the force of her amiable beauties in the recollection of a thousand tender passages that I coud wish to obliterate, till I am bid to revive them.—but experience alas! sadly reminds me how

Impossible this is.—and evinces an Opinion which I have long entertained, that there is a Destiny, which has the Sovereign controul of our Actions—not to be resisted by the strongest efforts of Human Nature.

You have drawn me my dear Madam, or rather have I drawn myself, into an honest confession of a Simple Fact—misconstrue not my meaning—'tis obvious—doubt it not, nor expose it,—the World has no business to know the object of my Love, declard in this manner to—you when I want to conceal it—

> Whatever the occasion, the same letter anticipated "the animating prospect of possessing Mrs. Custis,"[1] among the wealthiest women in Virginia. He married Martha Dandridge Custis a few months later. On the way to and from the front earlier in the spring he had courted Martha, a twenty-seven-year-old widow with two children, ages five and three, and legacy of about 6 million dollars. Her husband had left no will, so the courts divided the estate equally among her and the two children, Jacky and Patsy. Besides the New Kent County mansion called White House that neighbored a popular race course, she had a town house in Williamsburg where Washington had known her as belle of the ball, a buxom lass, about 5-feet-2-inches tall, with light-brown hair and dark eyes. Her plantations spread across six counties, and were worked by slaves valued at nine thousand pounds.[2] Marrying in White House (6 January 1759) they settled at Mount Vernon. Former aide George Mercer described the groom.

> *[Straight as an Indian, measuring 6 feet 2 inches in his stockings, and weighing 175 pounds. . . . His frame is padded with well-developed muscles, indicating great strength. His bones and joints are large as are his feet and hands. He is*

*wide shouldered, but has not a deep or round chest; is neat
waisted, but is broad across the hips, and has rather long legs
and arms. His head is well shaped though not large, but is
gracefully poised on a superb neck. A large and straight
rather than a prominent nose; blue-grey penetrating eyes
which are widely separated and overhung by a heavy brow.
His face is long rather than broad, with high round cheek
bones, and terminates in a good firm chin. He has a clear tho
rather colorless pale skin which burns with the sun.*

*A pleasing, benevolent, tho a commanding countenance,
dark brown hair which he wears in a cue. His mouth is large
and generally firmly closed, but which from time to time
discloses some defective teeth. His features are regular and
placid, with all the muscles of his face under perfect control,
tho flexible and expressive of deep feeling when moved by
emotions. In conversation he looks you full in the face, is
deliberate, deferential and engaging. His voice is agreeable
rather than strong. His demeanor at all times composed and
dignified. His movements and gestures are graceful, his walk
majestic, and he is a splendid horseman.]*[3]

Washington became responsible for managing the estate
that would take twenty years to unravel and a lifetime to
raise to his great expectations. Meanwhile, the newlyweds
settled at Mount Vernon with status just below regional
aristocracy but enhanced by his military fame and her
wealth. Besides social life in Williamsburg when courts
were in session, they had easy access to Belvoir and
recreation at nearby Alexandria so amusing that he
confided it to his diary.

Friday Feby 15th. Went to a Ball at Alexandria—where
Musick and Dancing was the chief Entertainment. However in a convenient Room detachd for the purpose

abounded plenty of Bread and Butter, some Biscuets with Tea, & Coffee which the Drinkers of coud not Distinguish from Hot water sweetned. Be it remembered that pocket handkerchiefs servd the purposes of Table Cloths & Napkins and that no Apologies were made for either. I shall therefore distinguish this Ball by the Stile & title of the Bread & Butter Ball.[4]

> In 1761, with the death of his brother Lawrence's widow, Washington inherited Mount Vernon outright. As country squire, he fulfilled his obligations to the community by serving as magistrate and in the local vestry and from 1759 in the House of Burgesses. There he continued fighting for justice due the military. A throat ailment made public speaking awkward, but he worked valiantly on committees or commissions and in preparing reports. His vocation, however, was making Mount Vernon proper for a country gentleman and his land productive enough to support the genteel living to which Martha Washington and an extended family had become accustomed.

Consider under what terrible management and disadvantages I found my Estate when I retired from the Publick Service of this Colony; and that besides some purchases of Lands and Negroes I was necessitated to make adjoining me—in order to support the Expences of a large Family—I had Provisions of all kinds to buy for the first two or three years, and my Plantation to Stock—in short with every thing—Buildings to make, and other matters, which swallowed up before I well knew where I was, all the money I got by Marriage nay more, brought me in Debt.[5]

> He ordered books on farming—Jethro Tull's *Horse-Hoeing Husbandry* and especially Edward Weston's *A New System of Agriculture; or, a Plain, Easy, and Demonstrative Method*

of speedily growing Rich (London 1755). Tobacco, the medium he used for English loans and goods, depleted the soil. He experimented with alfalfa, corn, wheat, and various grasses. He adopted the latest tools and techniques from English farmers, but their practices could not always adapt to Virginia's soil, heat, or droughts. Though often frustrated, as a pragmatist he felt confident that he could prevail with military "System and method."[6] He hedged his bet, however, with investments in land, forty-five hundred acres. They were worked by more than eighty-five slaves, who represented another problem for system and method. In Frederick County's smallpox epidemic of spring 1760, he took extra pains to protect them not as laborers only but as his "People."

Wednesday May 7. After taking the Doctor's Direction's in regard to my People I set out for my Quarters. . . . Engag'd Valentine Crawford to go in pursuit of a Nurse to be ready in case more of my People should be seizd with the same disorder.

Thursday May 8. Got Blankets and every other requisite from Winchester and settld things upon the best footing I coud to prevent the Small Pox from Spreading—and in case of its spreading for the care of the Negroes. Mr. Valentine Crawford agreeing in case any more of the People at the lower Quarter getting it to take them home to his House—and if any of those at the upper Quarter gets it to have them removd into my Room and the Nurse sent for.[7]

Notwithstanding the high risk, he invested in reclaiming primordial Dismal Swamp[8] and land on the frontier vulnerable to Indian raids. He pursued such ventures not for some abstract ideal of manifest destiny but as material foundation for his family's future among America's aristocracy of land. He advised friends to invest likewise.

Few there are I beleive, who woud choose to risque their money (unless influenced by motives of compassion) upon such hazardous & perishable Articles as Negroes, Stock, & Chattels, which are to be swept off by innumerable distempers, & subject to many accidents & misfortunes. . . . Discharge all your Debts, beginning with the Sales of such things as can be best spared, & so raising to Negroes, & even Land if requisite; for if the whole [economy] should go, there is a large Field before you—an opening prospect in the back Country for Adventurers—where numbers resort to—& where an enterprizing Man with very little Money may lay the foundation of a Noble Estate in the New Settlements upon Monongahela for himself and posterity. . . . [See] how the greatest Estates we have in this Colony were made; Was it not by taking up & purchasing at very low rates the rich back Lands which were thought nothing of in those days, but are now the most valuable Lands we possess? . . . Abiding where you are if you can save your Land & have a prospect of Reaping future advantages from it, or to remove back, where there is a moral certainty of laying the foundation of good Estates to your Children I say I woud but ask which of these two is the best.[9]

> In 1763 the Treaty of Paris ended French claims to western lands. Washington would speculate even more heavily in land grants to war veterans. An officer entitled to five thousand acres of his own, he nevertheless seemed obsessed with acquiring more and more, even engaging his younger brother Charles in duplicity for land's sake.[10]

Upon the whole, as you are situated in a good place [Fredericksburg] for seeing many of the Officers at different times, I should be glad if you woud (in a joking way, rather than in earnest at first) see what value they seem to set upon their Lands. . . . If you shoud make any purchases, let it be done in your own name; for reasons I shall give you when we meet.[11]

London merchants, however, proved to be his match in shady dealing. They would bring goods from England and take home shipments of tobacco. Washington depended on them for credit or hard money, either by loans or from sale of tobacco consigned to them. He depended on them also for such everyday necessities as clothing or hardware, even toys for the children's Christmas. Such solid dependence on them grew increasingly abrasive. Consignments of tobacco were normally subject to uncertainty of arrival and departure, acts of God, or neglect. With cynicism nurtured on the frontier, Washington suspected dishonesty and duplicity. He would complain to his London agent, Robert Cary and Company, with a veiled threat of taking his business elsewhere.

I do not like to recriminate on a Subject and shall therefore observe in few words, that Colonel Fairfax's Tobacco which Mr Athaws sold at 12 pence was no more than leaf, and of the same kind exactly with Numbers 15 and 16 of mine by the [ship] Unity [which sold at 11]; I coud conceive no reason therefore why his Tobacco shoud so far out sell mine, even that of York River [plantation] which has always been esteemed for its quality, however I shall dwell no longer on the matter, but rest perswaded that you will exert your best endeavours for my Interest, more especially as you must be sensible, that I have in a manner confined my correspondence to your House alone, and with this assurance, that I am not fond of change and want nothing but Justice—so long then as I meet with good Accounts and neighbourly fare I shall continue my Consignments, and farther I dare say you cannot expect.[12]

Flexing power of their own, Cary and Company countered by threatening to bypass Washington next year, leaving him anxious about how to ship his tobacco otherwise.[13]

Making matters worse in winter 1763, hard rains ruined his tobacco, corn, and wheat crops. Even worse, London merchants exerted pressure on the government to forbid colonists like him from using Virginia paper currency to pay overseas debts. Worst of all, in 1765 Parliament imposed the notorious Stamp Act, taxing paper that was vital to the business of everyday life. Coming in a season of agricultural depression, the new law triggered an explosive reaction to taxation without representation. Though a member of the House of Burgesses, Washington stayed home cultivating his gardens.[14] But a few months later, he abandoned olympian reserve to lobby Londoners with more pragmatic argument for repeal.

I may venture to affirm, that the advantage accrueing to the Mother Country will fall greatly short of the expectations of the Ministry; for certain it is, our whole Substance does already in a manner flow to Great Britain and that whatsoever contributes to lessen our Importation's must be hurtful to their Manufacturers—And the Eyes of our People—already beginning to open—will perceive, that many Luxuries which we lavish our substance to Great Britain for, can well be dispensd with whilst the necessaries of Life are (mostly) to be had within ourselves—This consequently will introduce frugality, and be a necessary stimulation to Industry.[15]

London merchants did obtain repeal of the Stamp Act but at the cost of the so-called Townshend Acts that in 1767 imposed duties on goods like tea, lead, paint, or glass and also ruled that Americans accused of treason had to stand trial in England. Though absent when the House of

Burgesses officially protested the new Acts, Washington worked with neighbor George Mason in developing the legislature's "resolves" asserting Virginians' sole right to tax themselves, protesting the change of venue for treason trials, and also proposing non-importation of British goods. Because Mason suffered crippling erysipelas, weak-voiced Washington introduced the "resolves" in the House of Burgesses in May 1769. Whether tempered by Mason or his own political sense, he repressed this earlier idea of using arms as last resort:

That no man shou'd scruple, or hesitate a moment to use a-ms in defence of so valuable a blessing, on which all the good and evil of life depends; is clearly my opinion; Yet A-ms I wou'd beg leave to add, should be the last resource; the dernier resort. Addresses to the Throne, and remonstrances to parliament, we have already, it is said, proved the inefficacy of; how far then their attention to our rights and priviledges is to be awakened or alarmed by starving their Trade and manufactures, remains to be tryed.

His enthusiasm for joining other colonies in a nonimportation agreement was also tempered by knowledge of human nature gained from living among the lowly on the frontier and from dealing with greedy land speculators and London merchants. He was prescient on intercolonial non-importation agreements of 1769.

The northern Colonies, it appears, are endeavouring to adopt this scheme—In my opinion it is a good one; & must be attended with salutary effects, provided it can be carried pretty generally into execution; but how far it is practicable to do so, I will not take upon me to determine. That there will be difficulties attending the execution of it every where, from clashing interests, and selfish designing men (ever attentive to their own gain, & watchful of every turn that can assist their lucrative views, in preference to any other consideration) cannot be denied.[16]

He was right. Non-importation agreements passed by the House of Burgesses in 1769 and in 1770 proved unenforceable and were ignored. In the early Seventies Washington was too busy to go with the flow of events creeping towards revolution. Lobbying for veterans' bounty had earned him more than twenty-four thousand acres of fine western land. Besides looking after far-flung properties and continuing to experiment with farming, he met the obligations of a patrician father by having Charles Willson Peale paint miniatures of the family and the well-known portrait of Washington in his militia colonel's red and black uniform complete with gorget and sash of office—in a pose that Napoleon one day would copy as tribute to his hero.

Washington became increasingly occupied with finding a system or plan for raising his adored stepchildren. Diary entries and correspondence over a half-dozen years (1768–1774) sound a litany of despair for Patsy's epilepsy and his irritation with Jacky, who was spoiled by a mother so indulgent that she could not stand to have him inoculated for smallpox; Washington had him innoculated without her knowing.

30 May 1768 [Jacky] is a boy of good genius, about 14 yrs of age, untainted in his Morals, and of innocent Manners . . . a promising boy—the last of his Family—and will possess a very large Fortune—add to this my anxiety to make him fit for more useful purposes, than a horse Racer etc.[17]

11 [June 1768] Sent for Doctor Rumney to [twelve-year old] Patcy Custis who was seized with fitts.

14 [April 1769] We set out to go to Captain McCartys

but Patcy being taken with a fit on the road by the Mill we turnd back.[18]

18 August 1769 About a fortnight ago I came to [Warmsprings] with Mrs Washington and her daughter, the latter of whom being troubled with a complaint, which the efficacy of these Waters it is thought might remove, we resolved to try them, but have found little benefit as yet from the experiment.

20 July 1770 Miss Custis's Complaint has been of two years standing, and rather Increases than abates.

16 December 1770 Jacky Custis now returns to [school at] Annapolis—His Mind a good deal relaxed from Study, & more than ever turnd to Dogs Horses & Guns; indeed upon Dress and equipage, which till of late, he has discoverd little Inclination of giving into. . . . I fear he will too soon think himself above controul, & be not much the better for the extraordinary expence attending his Living in Annapolis, which I shoud be exceeding sorry for, as nothing but a hasty progress towards the completion of his Education, can justifie my keeping him there.

20 April 1773 I shall say nothing further on the Subject [of Jacky's engagement to Nelly Calvert] than that I coud have wish'd he had postpond entering into the engagement till his Studies [at Columbia] were finishd, not that I have any objection to the Match, as she is a girl of exceeding good Character but because I fear, as he has discoverd [displayed] much fickleness already, that he may either change, and therefore injure the young Lady; or that it may precipitate him into a Marriage before, I am certain, he has ever bestowd a serious thought of the consequences; by which means his education is Interrupted, and he perhaps, wishing to be at liberty again before he is fairly imbarked on those important duties.

20 June 1773 It is an easier matter to conceive, than to describe, the distress of this Family . . . yesterday removd the Sweet Innocent Girl into a more happy, & peaceful abode than any she has met with, in the afflicted Path she hitherto has trod. She rose from Dinner about four Oclock, in better health and spirits than she appeard to have been in for some time; soon after which she was seizd with one of her usual Fits, and expird in it, in less than two Minutes without uttering a Word, a groan, or scarce a Sigh.[19]

As a measure of how much he suppressed private feelings from public view, the report of Patsy's death hid grief that was said to be so deep as to discourage Martha Washington from attending Jacky's wedding the next February. She is said to have sent a note: "God took from me a daughter when June roses were blooming—He has now given me another daughter, to warm my heart again. I am as happy as one so afflicted and so blest can be."[20]

Washington immersed himself in business—acting as agent for soldiers' land grants, speculating in ventures of his own, improving Mount Vernon, acting as executor for a half-dozen other estates, and managing Patsy Custis's share of her natural father's estate.

There has been scarce a Moment that I can properly call my own: For what with my own Business . . . together with the share I take in publick Affairs, constantly engaged in writing Letters—Settling Accounts—and Negotiating one piece of Business or another, in behalf of one or other of these Concerns; by which means I have really been deprivd of every kind of enjoyment, and had almost fully resolved to engage in no fresh matter, till I had entirely wound up the old.[21]

He was not so immersed in business as to ignore the tide swelling towards independence. With a passion for law and order and dependence on Atlantic commerce, he deplored the guerrilla action that dumped tea in Boston's harbor. He blamed Parliament for unlawfully closing Boston's port and restricting her government. He feared, in the summer of 1774, that "at the expence of Law and justice," Parliament had "a regular and systematic plan" to "overthrow our Constitutional Rights and liberties."[22] He added the pragmatism of experience to George Mason's more theoretical principles.

An Innate Spirit of freedom first told me, that the Measures are repugnant to every principle of natural justice ... not only repugnant to natural Right, but Subversive of the Laws & Constitution of Great Britain itself; in the Establishment of which some of the best Blood in the Kingdom hath been Spilt; Satisfied then that the Acts of a British Parliament are no longer Govern'd by the Principles of justice—that it is trampling upon the Valuable Rights of American's, confirmd to them by Charter, and the Constitution they themselves boast of; and convinc'd beyond the smallest doubt, that these Measures are the result of deliberation; and attempted to be carried into Execution by the hand of Power is it a time to trifle, or risk our Cause upon Petitions which with difficulty obtain access, and afterwards are thrown by with the utmost contempt—or should we, because hitherto unsuspicious of design and then unwilling to enter into disputes with the Mother Country go on to bear more, and forbear to innumerate our just causes of Complaint. . . . I could wish, I own, that the dispute had been left to Posterity to determine, but the Crisis is arrivd when we must assert our Rights, or Submit to every Imposition that can be heap'd upon us; till custom and use, will make us as tame, and abject Slaves, as the Blacks we Rule over with such arbitrary Sway.[23]

He and Mason once again worked out a program for Washington to present to the House of Burgesses. They enumerated grievances asserting the constitutional rights of colonials to govern themselves in internal affairs. Virginia subsequently held a ratifying convention at which Patrick Henry is supposed to have appealed for liberty or death and Washington to have made the startling promise: "I will raise 1000 Men, subsist them at my own Expence, and march my self at their Head for the Relief of Boston."[24] As the local squire, he did spend 150 pounds for forty muskets, 50 pounds more for accessories, and a guinea for military manuals.

Popularly elected one of Virginia's seven delegates to the first Continental Congress, he sallied forth to Philadelphia. There he took no part in debates, but feted that summer as a military hero, he made no secret of committing to the Glorious Cause.

I think I can announce it as a fact, that it is not the wish, or the interest of the Government, or any other upon this Continent, separately, or collectively, to set up for Independence; but . . . none of them will ever submit to the loss of those valuable rights and priviledges which are essential to the happiness of every free State, and without which, Life, Liberty and property are rendered totally insecure.[25]

In the six months between First and Second Continental Congresses, Washington managed Mount Vernon and western lands, and yet devoted much time to training county militia and stockpiling ammunition until hearing about bloodshed at Concord and Lexington, 19 April 1775. He had prepared his mind for the inevitable consequences.

Unhappy it is to reflect, that a Brother's Sword has been sheathed in a Brother's breast, and that, the once happy and peaceful plains of America are either to be drenched with Blood, or Inhabited by Slaves. Sad alternative! But can a virtuous Man hesitate in his choice?[26]

5

WAGING WAR

1775–1781

In May of 1775, at the Second Continental Congress, Washington served on committees that organized intercolonial government and a military force. Dressing in his Virginia colonel's uniform signaled his willingness to command, but because of regional power plays, he was not the unanimous choice until John Adams, representing Massachusetts, made an impassioned speech nominating him. Later, Adams would say, "Mr. Washington, who happened to sit near the Door, as soon as he heard me allude to him, from his Usual Modesty darted into the Library Room."[1] On 15 June 1775, he was unanimously elected at salary of $500 dollars, or 150 pounds, a month for pay and expenses. The following day, he told Congress he would serve for expenses only, projecting sincere modesty in risking fame, fortune, and freedom for American independence.

Tho' I am truly sensible of the high Honour done me in this Appointment, yet I feel great distress from a consciousness that my abilities and Military experience may not be equal to the extensive and important Trust: However, as the Congress desire I will enter upon the momentous duty, and exert every power I Possess In their Service for the Support of the glorious Cause. . . .

But lest some unlucky event should happen unfavourable to my reputation, I beg it may be remembered by every Gentleman in the room, that I this day declare with the utmost sincerity, I do not think my self equal to the Command I am honoured with.

As to pay, Sir, I beg leave to Assure the Congress that as no pecuniary consideration could have tempted me to have accepted this Arduous emploiment at the expence of my domestik ease and happiness I do not wish to make any proffit from it: I will keep an exact Account of my expences; those I doubt not they will discharge and that is all I desire.[2]

> Privately, he rationalized his reluctant acceptance to
> Martha Washington (using her pet name, "Patcy") as
> somehow predestined.

It has been determined in Congress, that the whole Army raised for the defence of the American Cause shall be put under my care, and that it is necessary for me to proceed immediately to Boston to take upon me the Command of it. You may beleive me my dear Patcy, when I assure you, in the most solemn manner, that, so far from seeking this appointment I have used every endeavour in my power to avoid it, not only from an unwillingness to part with you and the Family, but from a consciousness of it being a trust too great for my Capacity and that I should enjoy more real happiness and felicity in one month with you, at home, than I have the most distant prospect of reaping abroad, if my stay was to be Seven times Seven years. But, as it has been a kind of destiny that has thrown me upon this Service, I shall hope that my undertaking of it, is designd to answer some good purpose.

You might, and I suppose did perceive, from the Tenor of my letters, that I was apprehensive I could not avoid this appointment, as I did not even pretend to intimate when I should return—that was the case—it was utterly out of my power to refuse this appointment without exposing my Character to such censures as would have reflected dishonour upon myself, and given pain to my friends— this I am sure could not, and ought not to be pleasing to you, and must have lessend me considerably in my own esteem. I shall rely therefore, confidently, on that Providence which has heretofore preservd, and been bountiful to me, not doubting but that I shall return safe to you in the fall— I shall feel no pain from the Toil, or the danger of the Campaign—My unhappiness will flow, from the uneasiness I know you will feel at being left alone—I therefore beg of you to summon your whole Fortitude & Resolution, and pass your time as agreeably as possible—nothing will give me so much sincere satisfaction as to hear this, and to hear it from your own Pen. . . . [3]

> In mid-December, along with Jacky Custis and Jacky's pregnant wife, Martha would join him at his Cambridge headquarters. On the way, she too was lavishly entertained "in as great pomp as if I had been a very great somebody."[4] She would stay with him in subsequent winters as at Valley Forge, his hostess, nurse, and copyist. During their absences, Mount Vernon would be managed by cousin Lund Washington but with General Washington routinely advising, consenting, and sometimes grumbling—as when Lund offered hospitality to enemy raiders.

To go on board their Vessels; carry them refreshments; commune with a parcel of plundering Scoundrels, and request a favor by asking the surrender of [20 stolen] Negroes, was exceedingly ill-judged, and 'tis to be feared, will be unhappy in its consequences, as it will be a precedent for others, and may become the subject of animadversion.[5]

On 23 June 1775, he sent Martha Washington a farewell note from Philadelphia trusting in Providence and friends.

As I am within a few minutes of leaving this City, I could not think of departing from it without dropping you a line; especially as I do not know whether it may be in my power to write again till I get to the Camp at Boston—I go fully trusting in that Providence, which has been more bountiful to me than I deserve, and in full confidence of a happy meeting with you sometime in the Fall—I have not time to add more, as I am surrounded with Company to take leave of me—I retain an unalterable affection for you, which neither time or distance can change. . . .[6]

Before leaving Philadelphia he had drawn plans for organizing the troops, but at Boston he discovered that he had been deceived about their quality.

Their Officers generally speaking are the most indifferent kind of People I ever saw. I have already broke one Colonel and five Captains for cowardice, and for drawing more Pay and Provisions than they had Men in their Companies . . . in short they are by no means such Troops, in any respect, as you are led to believe of them from the Accounts which are published, but I need not make myself Enemies among them, by this declaration, though it is consistent with truth. I daresay the Men would fight very well (if properly Officered) although they are an exceeding dirty and nasty people.[7]

A year later, on 30 September 1776, he was in despair. Congress rejected his call for a regular, standing army, relying instead on state militias serving for a few months, at most a year. Militiamen became the butt of jokes like the trooper who single-handedly brings in a squad of prisoners. When General Washington asks how he captured so many by himself, he replies, "By Jasus, I surrounded them."[8] They were no joke to Washington, who would find that even when troops were at full strength on paper he could account for barely a third of them.[9]

You have had great bodies of militia in pay that never were in camp. . . . Your stores have been expended, and every kind of military discipline destroyed by them; your numbers fluctuating, uncertain, and forever far short of report. . . . I discharged a regiment the other day that had in it fourteen rank and file fit for duty only, and several that had less than fifty. In short, such is my situation that if I were to wish the bitterest curse to an enemy this side of the grave, I should put him in my stead with my feelings; and yet I do not know what plan of conduct to pursue.

I see the impossibility of serving with reputation, or doing any essential service to the cause by continuing in command, and yet I am told that if I quit the command inevitable ruin will follow from the distraction that will ensue. . . . I never was in such an unhappy, divided state since I was born. . . . I am wearied to death all day with a variety of perplexing circumstances.[10]

As he had struggled in Virginia for equitable treatment for his men, so now he sustained a running battle with Congress not just for pay but for such bare essentials as food and clothing. He tried what he could to mend matters with regular subservient reports to each governor, as well as to the impotent Congress. He had continual consultation with officers and issued daily information and exhortation to troops by means of General Orders. On 1 August 1776, he appealed to them to put aside regional differences for the sake of their common cause, as he himself did in appointing equitably commanders and aides from each state.

That the Honor and Success of the army, and the safety of our bleeding Country, depends upon harmony and good agreement with each other; That the Provinces are all United to oppose the common enemy, and all distinctions sunk in the name of an American; to make this honorable, and pre-serve the Liberty of our Country, ought to be our only emu-lation, and he will be the best Soldier, and the best Patriot, who contributes most to this glorious work, whatever his Station, or from whatever part of the Continent, he may come: Let all distinctions of Nations, Countries, and Prov-inces therefore be lost in the generous contest, who shall behave with the most Courage against the enemy, and the most kindness and good humour to each other.[11]

The aides he appointed offered an unplanned benefit by making up a pool of such potential leaders as Alexander Hamilton and by forming an interstate network of mutual support and friendship. In the field, the young men could also provide him with recreation, as when inviting officers' wives to lunch at the General's table.

Since our arrival . . . ,we have had a Ham (sometimes a shoulder) of Bacon, to grace the head of the table; a piece of roast Beef adorns the foot; and a small dish of Greens or Beans (almost imperceptable) decorates the center.

When the Cook has a mind to cut a figure . . . we have two Beefstake-Pyes, or dishes of Crabs in addition, one on each side the center dish, dividing the space, and reducing the distance between dish and dish to about Six feet, which without them, would be near twelve apart. Of late he has had the surprizing luck to discover, that apples will make pyes; and it's a question if, amidst the violence of his efforts, we do not get one of apples instead of having both of Beef.[12]

Compared to the futility of influencing Congress, Washington found it much easier to win respect from British officials sent to pacify the rebels. Lord Richard Howe had tried to broker a peaceful settlement with Benjamin Franklin in London. He was a wise choice, being the younger brother of an American hero who had died fighting the French at Ticonderoga. Another brother, however, was General Sir William Howe, who was commanding the British at Boston. In dealing with them, Washington subdued his usual modesty, abandoned deference to aristocracy, and boldly asserted himself their equal.

In mid-July 1776, Lord Richard Howe sought a conference at Staten Island. He addressed his letter to "George Washington Esqr. etc.—etc.—"[13] Washington, in line with a policy of participatory democracy, counseled with his officers. When Lord Howe sent a colonel as emissary, Washington appointed a colonel to negotiate with him. Since the message violated propriety, Washington could not receive it.

I immediately convened such of the General officers who were not upon other duty who agreed in opinion that I ought not to receive any Letter directed to me as a private Gentleman, but if otherwise and the Officer desired to come up to deliver the Letter himself as was suggested, he should come under a safe conduct. Upon this I directed Colonel [Joseph] Reed to go down and manage the affair under the above general Instruction.

On his return he Informed me, after the common civilities the Officer acquainted him that he had a Letter from Lord Howe to Mr Washington which he shewed under a superscription to George Washington Esqr.

Colonel Reed replied there was no such person in the Army and that a Letter Intended for the General could not be received under such a direction.

The Officer expressed great concern, said It was a Letter rather of a civil than Military nature. That Lord Howe regretted he had not arrived sooner. That he (Lord Howe) had great Powers. The anxiety to have the Letter received was very evident, though the Officer disclaimed all Knowledge of Its contents. However Colonel Reed's Instructions being positive they parted.

Washington's official report omitted the wry repartee reported by Dr. James Thacher.

[Colonel James Paterson again waited on General Washington and on this occasion he addressed him by the title of Excellency . . . and assured him that they had the highest personal respect for General Washington, and did not mean to derogate from his rank; that the letter, of which he was now the bearer from the [peace] Commissioners, was directed to George Washington, Esq., etc. etc. etc. which they hoped would remove all difficulties; as the three et ceteras might be understood to imply every thing that ought to follow. To this the general replied, that though it was true the three et ceteras might mean every thing, it was also true they might mean any thing.][14]

Washington believed his mission had divine sanction. He reminded old comrade Adam Stephen why they were back in the saddle again. They had prevailed over the French in 1754 and 1755 and now ought to expect the same dispensation since they fought for a more glorious cause.

I did not let the Anniversary of the 3d or 9th of [July] pass of without a grateful remembrance of the escape we had at the Meadows and on the Banks of the Monongahela.

The same Providence that protected us upon those occasions will, I hope, continue his Mercies, and make us happy Instruments in restoring Peace and liberty to this once favour'd, but now distressed Country.[15]

> They needed all the help they could get. Vicious fighting spread along the western and northern frontiers. The British attacked in superior numbers from all sides and along the shores. European-style siege warfare worked in the early days at Boston. But, grounded on experience, Washington learned by trial and error that his troops were better suited to guerrilla-style surprise raids as in the celebrated crossing of the Delaware on Christmas Eve 1776.
>
> Against twelve hundred Hessians, Washington massed two thousand troops, but it was nature that made the difference. Freezing weather hindered the bulky Gloucester fishing boats, limiting the number of troops that could cross. Washington realized that the reduced number gained mobility. Smaller brigades, each supported by artillery companies, caught the Hessians at dawn hungover from Christmas revelry, their officers still abed.

The quantity of Ice, made that Night, impeded the passage of the Boats so much, that it was three OClock before the Artillery could all be got over, and near four, before the Troops took up their line of march. This made me despair of surprizing the Town, as I well knew we could not reach it before the day was fairly broke but as I was certain there was no making a Retreat without being discovered, and harassed on repassing the River, I determined to push on at all Events. . . . We presently saw their main body formed, but from their Motions, they seem'd undetermined how to act. . . .

Finding from our disposition, that they were surrounded, and that they must inevitably be cut to peices if they made any further Resistance, they agreed to lay down their Arms. The Number, that submitted in this manner, was 23 Officers and 886 Men. Colonel [Johan] Rall the commanding Officer and seven others were found wounded in the Town. I dont exactly know how many they had killed, but I fancy not above twenty or thirty, as they never made any regular Stand.[16]

> The next year, General Horatio Gates used similar tactics to defeat General John Burgoyne at Saratoga by seducing him to stretch supply lines until too fatigued to fight. Later, Nathanael Greene would do the same to Lord Cornwallis in the Carolinas. But in a war wearing down friend and foe, Washington found it hard to blame losses on Providence, or Nature, or human error. A sortie at Germantown must have felt déjà vu when there rolled in a fog so dense that his men (as they had in the dark forest twenty years earlier) fired blindly at one another.[17]

A thick Fog rendered so infinitely dark at times, as not to distinguish friend from Foe at the distance of 30 Yards . . . Providence or some unaccountable something, designed it [that] after we had driven the Enemy a Mile or two, after they were in the utmost confusion, and flying before us in most places, after we were upon the point (as it appeard to every body) of grasping a compleat Victory, our own Troops took fright and fled with precipitation and disorder.

How to account for this, I know not, unless, as I before observed, the Fog represented their own Friends to them for a Reinforcement of the Enemy as we attacked in different Quarters at the same time, and were about closing the Wings of our Army when this happened.[18]

> And where was Providence during the mild winter of 1777–1778? General Howe staged lavish parties in Phila-

delphia while Washington and his troops at Valley Forge barely scraped by on improvised food and shelter. Morale improved in May when Franklin persuaded France to recognize American independence with ships, men, and materiel. Washington relied on providential aid to counter the human errors of generals, as when irascible General Charles Lee, on the verge of victory, retreated without telling his men what he was doing.

The disorder arising from it would have proved fatal to the Army had not that bountiful Providence which has never failed us in the hour of distress, enabled me to form a Regiment or two (of those that were retreating) in the face of the Enemy, and under their fire, by which means a stand was made long enough (the place through which the enemy were pursuing being narrow) to form the Troops that were advancing, upon an advantageous piece of Ground in the rear. Hence our affairs took a favourable turn, and from being pursued, we drove the Enemy back. . . .

As the event unfolded, Washington once more must have felt the sense of déjà vu, it was a replay of his march twenty years earlier to attack Fort Duquesne only to find that the French had abandoned it.

In the Morning we expected to renew the Action, when behold the enemy had stole off as Silent as the Grave in the Night.[19]

More painful was the betrayal by one of his favorite generals, Benedict Arnold, who tried to sell out West Point to British spy Major John Andre. Washington confessed he had no suspicion till Arnold defected "and then he could trace back and see through his intentions from the beginning."[20] This was not true of seeing through Mrs. Arnold. When he arrived at West Point, he found himself comforting beautiful Peggy Arnold, confined to bed, unaware that she, an unindicted conspirator, was only feigning hysteria at her husband's flight.[21]

A military tribunal sentenced Andre to hang. Washington did not interfere. In contrast to keeping Christopher Gist from killing the Indian who shot at them on the frontier, Washington ordered death for wartime crimes. Mutiny, however, presented a special case. When in January 1781 Pennsylvania regular troops marched on Congress, Washington sympathized with them. He worried about the immediate effect on other restless troops, of course, but also the long range consequences if Congress and the states did not redress the soldiers' grievances.

The aggravated calamities and distresses that have resulted, from the total want of pay for nearly twelve Months, for want of cloathing, at a severe season, and not unfrequently the want of provisions; are beyond description. The circumstances will now point out much more forcibly what ought to be done, than any thing that can possibly be said by me, on the subject. . . . It is in vain to think an Army can be kept together much longer, under such a variety of sufferings as ours has experienced: and that unless some immediate and spirited measures are adopted to furnish at least three Months pay to the Troops, in Money that will be of some value to them; And at the same time ways and means are devised to cloath and feed them better (more regularly I mean) than they have been, the worst that can befall us may be expected.[22]

After Congress negotiated compromise, Washington felt that he could not override their authority. But when, within weeks, two hundred New Jersey mutineers marched on Trenton seeking similar redress, Washington had two ringleaders shot to prevent mutiny from spreading further. He blamed the hopeless state of affairs not on Providence but on human nature that had devised the confederated form of government in which each state was sovereign and Congress had power only on paper.

It must be a settled plan, founded on System, order and economy that is to carry us triumphantly through the war. Supiness, and an indifference to the distresses and cries of a sister State when danger is far off, and a general but momentary resort to arms when it comes to our doors, are equally impolitic and dangerous, and proves the necessity of a controuling power in Congress to regulate and direct all matters of *general* concern; without it the great business of war never can be well conducted, if it can be conducted at all: while the powers of Congress are only recommendatory; while one State yields obedience, and another refuses it; while a third mutilates and adopts the measure in part only, and all vary in time and manner, it is scarcely possible our affairs should prosper, or that any thing but disappointment can follow the best concerted plans. . . . A nominal head, which at present is but another name for Congress, will no longer do. That honorable body, after hearing the interests and views of the several States fairly discussed and explained by their respective representatives, must dictate, not merely recommend, and leave it to the States afterwards to do as they please, which, as I have observed before, is in many cases, to do nothing at all.[23]

> Experience following surrender at Great Meadow had taught him the power of purloined papers for propaganda. Now, in August of 1781, apparently scheming to leak disinformation about attacking New York, he noted in his journal that the attack had been foiled by the States' negligence.

My heavy ordnance and Stores from the Eastward had also come on to the North River and every thing would have been in perfect readiness to commense the operation against New York, if the States had furnished their quotas of men agreeably to my requisitions.[24]

Seven years later, he confessed the plan was a hoax to deceive the enemy.

It was determined by me (nearly twelve months before hand) at all hazards to give out and cause it to be believed by the highest military as well as civil Officers that New York was the destined place of attack, for the important purpose of inducing the Eastern and Middle States to make greater exertions in furnishing specific supplies than they otherwise would have done, as well as for the interesting purpose of rendering the enemy less prepared elsewhere.... For I repeat it, and dwell upon it again and again—some splendid advantage (whether upon a larger or smaller scale was almost immaterial) was so essentially necessary to revive the expiring hopes and languid exertions of the Country, at the crisis in question, that I never would have consented to embark in any enterprize, wherein, from the most rational plan & accurate calculations, the favourable issue should not have appeared as clear to my view, as a ray of light. The failure of an attempt against the Posts of the enemy, could, in no other possible situation during the war, have been so fatal to our cause.

That much trouble was taken and finesse used to misguide & bewilder Sir Henry Clinton in regard to the real object, by fictitious communications ... is certain. Nor were less pains taken to deceive our own Army; for I had always conceived, when the imposition did not completely take place at home, it could never sufficiently succeed abroad.[25]

The decision to attack New York would have been a bad plan. The French general Jean Comte de Rochambeau, with five thousand polished troops at Dobbs Ferry, joined François Comte de Grasse, admiral of the West Indies fleet, in persuading him instead to march to the Chesapeake where de Grasse would rout the British fleet supporting Cornwallis at Yorktown. As Washington marched southward, he was able to spend a few days at Mount Vernon, his first visit in over six years.

Martha Washington, sensing the war's end, had finally allowed twenty-eight-year-old Jacky to volunteer at Yorktown. Within two weeks, on 5 November 1781, he was dead from camp fever, leaving four children, the eldest only five years old. Like that of Patcy Custis earlier, his death devastated both Washingtons.

I arrived ... time enough to see poor Mr. Custis breathe his last; this unexpected and affecting event threw Mrs. Washington and Mrs. Custis (who were both present) into such deep distress, that the circumstances of it and a duty I owed the decease in assisting at his funeral rights prevented my [returning to duty].[26]

At the beginning of the war, Washington had insisted that Lord Howe respect his rank. Now when Cornwallis, feigning illness, sent his second-in-command, General Charles O'Hara, to surrender the British troops, Washington insisted that his own second-in-command, General Benjamin Lincoln, receive them. It would take another two years for the British to give up New York and go home.

6

A FAREWELL TO ARMS

1781–1784

Fighting continued for two years along the western frontier against Indian allies of the British. Treaty negotiations dragged on in Paris while Washington's troops in camp became edgy from inactivity. He suspected the British of delaying peace in hopes that the American army would defect or disband.

It really appears, from the conduct of the States, that they do not conceive it necessary for the Army to receive any thing but hard knocks; to give them pay is a matter which has been long out of the question and we were upon the very point of trying our hand at how we could live without subsistence. . . . Our Horses have long been without every thing their own thriftiness could not supply. Let any Man, who will allow reason fair play, ask himself what must be the inevitable consequences of such policy.[1]

His own patience had been long strained.

I can say, with much truth, that there is not a Man in America that more fervently wishes for Peace, and a return to private life than I do. Nor will any man go back to the rural and domestick enjoyments of it with more Heart felt pleasure than I shall.[2]

———

As Washington himself a generation earlier, some officers tired of rejected petitions and called for action. In his heart, he sympathized. "We must," he allowed, "take human nature as we find it."[3] But at Newburgh headquarters he suspected outside agents were provoking the unrest.

Such sentiments as these were immediately and industriously circulated: That it was universally expected the Army would not disband until they had obtained Justice.... That some Members of Congress wished the Measure might take effect, in order to compel the Public, particularly the delinquent States, to do justice. With many other Suggestions of a Similar Nature; from whence, and a variety of other considerations it is generally believ'd the Scheme was not only planned, but also digested and matured in Philadelphia and . . . as soon as the Minds of the Army were thought to be prepared for the transaction, anonymous invitations were circulated, requesting a general Meeting of the Officers next day.[4]

Unannounced, Washington attended the officers' meeting. He made a dramatic appeal for their continuing loyalty to Congress, fumbling for his reading glasses, mumbling so all could hear: "I have not only grown gray but almost blind in the service of my country."[5]

The threat may have been exaggerated, but his performance calmed the men. More important, it defused military intervention in politics. A week later, a frightened Congress promised pensions of five years' full pay for the officers. Washington had heard promises before. Again, the real problem lay in the Confederation itself, impotent to compel the states to pay their fair share.

If the States will not furnish the Supplies required by

Congress, thereby enabling the Superintendant of Finance to feed, clothe, and pay the army; if they suppose the war can be carried on without money, or that money can be borrowed without permanent funds to pay the interest on it; if they have no regard to justice, because it is attended with expence; if gratitude to men, who have rescued them from the jaws of danger and brought them to the haven of Independence and Peace, is to subside, as danger is removed . . . If such, I say, should be the sentiments of the States; and that their conduct, or the conduct of some, does but too well warrant the conclusion, well may another anonymous addresser step forward, and with more effect than the last did, say with him, "You have arms in your hands, do justice to yourselves, and never sheath the sword, 'till you have obtained it."[6]

In April 1783 the preliminary treaty of peace recognized American independence. Two months later, Washington addressed a circular letter to each state's governor announcing his retirement from the army in terms prefiguring his more celebrated Farewell Address of 1796. Disclaiming personal ambition, he repeated the call for remodeling the Confederation.

This is the favorable moment to give such a tone to our Federal Government, as will enable it to answer the ends of its institution, or this may be the ill-fated moment for relaxing the powers of the Union, annihilating the cement of the Confederation, and exposing us to become the sport of European politics, which may play one State against another to prevent their growing importance, and to serve their own interested purposes. For, according to the system of Policy the States shall adopt at this moment, they will stand or fall, and by their confirmation or lapse, it is yet to be decided, whether the Revolution must ultimately be considered as a blessing or a curse: a blessing or a curse, not to the present age alone, for with our fate will the destiny of unborn Millions be involved.

> He went on to urge strong central authority, sound public credit, a standing army, and a moral crusade that would reshape human nature on the model of Jesus.

I now make it my earnest prayer, that God would have you, and the State over which you preside, in his holy protection, that he would incline the hearts of the Citizens to cultivate a spirit of subordination and obedience to Government, to entertain a brotherly affection and love for one another, for their fellow Citizens of the United States at large, and particularly for their brethren who have served in the Field, and finally, that he would most graciously be pleased to dispose us all, to do Justice, to love mercy, and to demean ourselves with that Charity, humility and pacific temper of mind, which were the Characteristicks of the Divine Author of our blessed Religion, and without an humble imitation of whose example in these things, we can never hope to be a happy Nation.[7]

> Before Washington could retire, he had to wait until September for the arrival of the Treaty of Paris that ended the war and then for the British to leave New York.
> "Endeavouring to stifle the feelings of Joy in his own bosom," Washington chose the anniversary of the fight at Lexington to proclaim the end of fighting—as if bringing down the curtain on the last scene of a play.

Nothing now remains but for the actors of this mighty Scene to preserve a perfect, unvarying consistency of character through the very last act; to close the Drama with applause; and to retire from the Military Theatre with the same approbation of Angells and men which have crowned all their former vertuous Actions.[8]

> While waiting for the British to leave New York City (on 23 November 1783) Washington toured the eastern states, exploring the vast inland waterways surely with an eye to post-retirement investments.

I shall not rest contented 'till I have explored the Western Country, and traversed those lines (or great part of them) which have given bounds to a New Empire. But when it may, if it ever shall happen, I dare not say, as my first attention must be given to the deranged situation of my private concerns which are not a little injured by almost nine years absence and total disregard of them.[9]

> He also now had time to worry about his extended family's affairs. His seventy-five-year-old mother had been telling people that her celebrated son shamefully neglected her, leaving her dependent on the kindness of strangers. Washington harshly denied the allegation.

I learn from very good authority that she is upon all occasions, and in all Companies complaining of the hardness of the times—of her wants and distresses; and if not in direct terms, at least by strong innuendos inviting favors which not only makes *her* appear in an unfavourable point of view but *those* also who are connected with her. That she can have no *real* wants that may not be supplied I am sure of—*imaginary* wants are indefinite, and oftentimes insatiable, because they are boundless and always changing.[10]

> She has had a great deal of money from me at times . . . and over and above this has not only had all that was ever made from the Plantation but got her provisions and every thing else she thought proper from thence. In short to the best of my recollection I have never in my life received a

copper from the estate—and have paid many hundred pounds (first and last) to her in cash—[11]

He now also had time to counsel his twenty-one-year-old nephew, Bushrod Washington, who was about to study law in Philadelphia, on living in the big city.

[Remember] that the Company in which you will improve most, will be least expensive to you; and yet I am not such a Stoic as to suppose you will, or to think it right that you ought, always to be in Company with Senators and Philosophers; but, of the Young and Juvenile kind, let me advise you to be choice. It is easy to make acquaintances, but very difficult to shake them off; however irksome and unprofitable they are found, after we have once committed ourselves to them; the indiscretions and scrapes, which very often they involuntarily lead one into, proves equally distressing and disgraceful.[12]

Finally, at noon on 4 December 1783, Fraunces Tavern provided the backdrop for the celebrated theatrical scene in which Washington said farewell to several of his officers. Choked up, unable to speak, he embraced first robust Henry Knox, then each in turn. He took a triumphal journey to Annapolis, the temporary seat of Congress, on 23 December, to relinquish his commission.

So magnanimous an act at the height of power did not surprise those who had suffered with him the unrelenting stress of an eight-year struggle against foes foreign and domestic. The British had fallen, but the Confederation system remained intact. As a pragmatist, he had tried to work with the system. Now as the external threat relaxed, he could bow off the stage with clear conscience to the applause of the world. He could do no more.

Having finished the work assigned me, I retire from the

great theatre of Action; and bidding an Affectionate farewell to this August body under whose orders I have so long acted, I here offer my Commission, and take leave of all the employments of public life.[13]

7

SEEKING RETIREMENT

1784–1786

Except for the brief visit on the way to Yorktown, Washington had not been home for eight years. He estimated that his absence had cost him ten thousand pounds. Still, he was in good shape (a muscular two hundred pounds on a six-foot-two frame) and looked forward to the pleasures of retiring under his own vine and fig tree. He and Martha Washington, now in their fifties, took the two younger children left by Jacky Custis to raise as their own—bright-eyed five-year-old Nelly and three-year-old George Washington Custis, familiarly known as "Wash" or "Tub."

At length I am now become a private citizen on the banks of the Potomac, and under the shadow of my own Vine and my own Fig tree, free from the bustle of a camp and the busy scenes of public life. . . . I am not only retired from all public employments, but I am retireing within myself; and shall be able to view the solitary walk, and tread the paths of private life with heartfelt satisfaction. Envious of none, I am determined to be pleased with all, and this being the order for my march, I will move gently down the stream of life, until I sleep with my Fathers.[1]

He underestimated his celebrity as world-class hero.

Martha Washington's niece, Fanny Bassett, came to live with them as a daughter at fifteen. She soon shared her aunt's duties as hostess, looking after the unending parade of family, friends, and curiosity seekers from America and overseas on pilgrimage to Mount Vernon. Washington escaped by riding off to look after the properties and getting used to unfamiliar freedom.

I am just beginning to experience that ease, and freedom from public cares which, however desirable, takes some time to realize; for strange as it may tell, it is nevertheless true, that it was not till lately I could get the better of my usual custom of ruminating as soon as I waked in the Morning, on the business of the ensuing day; and of my surprize, after having revolved many things in my mind, to find that I was no longer a public Man, or had any thing to do with public transactions.

I feel now, however, as I conceive a wearied Traveller must do, who, after treading many a painful step, with a heavy burden on his Shoulders, is eased of the latter, having reached the Goal to which all the former were directed— and from his House top is looking back, and tracing with a grateful eye the Meanders by which he escaped the quicksands and Mires which lay in his way, and into which none but the All-powerful guide, and great disposer of human Events could have prevented his falling.[2]

Once his metabolism adjusted to civilian life, he tried micromanaging every detail of his farms, rebuilding and renovating Mount Vernon. But fame proved relentless. Besides the streams of pilgrims seeking sight of the "Saviour of His Country,"[3] familiar and strange supplicants sought testimony or testimonials. They all put a premium on his time. Britisher John Hunter, arriving in November of 1785, left detailed notes of the routine.

[His greatest pride now is, to be thought the first farmer in America. He is quite a Cincinnatus, and often works with his men himself—strips off his coat and labors like a common man. The General has a great turn for mechanics. It's astonishing with what niceness he directs everything in the building way, condescending even to measure the thing himself, that all may be perfectly uniform. . . . His eyes are full and blue and seem to express an air of gravity. His nose inclines to the aquiline; his mouth small; his teeth are yet good and his cheeks indicate perfect health. His forehead is a noble one and he wears his hair turned back, without curls and in the officer's style, and tyed in a long queue behind. . . . People come to see him here from all parts of the world—hardly a day passes without; but the General seldom makes his appearance before dinner; employing the morning to write his letters and superintend his farm, and allotting the afternoon to company; but even then he generally retires for two hours between tea and supper to his study to write. . . . He keeps as regular Books as any Merchant whatever, and a daily Journal of all his transactions. It's amazing the number of letters he wrote during the war: there are thirty large folio volumes of them upstairs, as big as common Ledgers, all neatly copied. . . .][4]

At no period of the war have I been obliged to write half as much as I now do, from necessity. . . . What with letters (often of an unmeaning nature) from foreigners. Enquiries after Dick, Tom, and Harry who *may have been* in some part, or at *sometime*, in the Continental service. Letters, or certificates of service for those who want to go out of their own State. Introductions; applications for copies of Papers; references of a thousand old matters with which I *ought* not to be troubled more than the Great Mogul, but which must receive an answer of some kind, deprive me of my usual exercise; and without relief, may be injurious to me as I already begin to feel the weight, and oppression of it in my head, and am assured by the *faculty*, if I do not change my course, I shall certainly sink under it.[5]

He had every intention of organizing his papers, official and personal, a great mass considering that his habit was to save copies of all correspondence, public or private, with multiple copies of official letters—one to recipient, one to file, others in case of loss in transit. Congress would even pay to help organize the official papers.

I intended to have devoted the present expiring winter in arranging all my papers which I had left at home, and which I found a mere mass of confusion (occasioned by frequently shifting them into trunks, and suddenly removing them from the reach of the enemy)—but however strange it may seem it is nevertheless true, that what with company; referrences of old matters with which I ought not to be troubled—applications for certificates, and copies of orders, in addition to the routine of letters which have multiplied greatly upon me; I have not been able to touch a single paper, or transact any business of my own, in a way of accounts etc. during the whole course of the winter; or in a word, since my retirement from public life.[6]

William Gordon spent three weeks at Mount Vernon copying Washington's public papers for a history of the revolution. But Washington refused John Bowie who wanted to separate the public General from the private George Washington.

I found that this must be a very futile work (if under *any* circumstances it could be made interesting) unless he could be furnished with the incidents of my life, either from my papers or my recollection, and digesting of past transactions into some sort of form and order with respect to times and circumstances: I knew also that many of the former relative to the part I had acted in the war between France and Great Britain from the year 1754, until the peace of Paris; and which contained some of the most interesting occurrences of my life, were lost; that my memory is too treacherous to be relied on to supply this defect; and, admitting both were more perfect, that submitting such a publication to the world whilst I continue on the theater, might be ascribed (however involuntarily I was led into it) to vain motives.[7]

Any memoirs of my life, distinct and unconnected with the general history of the war would rather hurt my feelings than tickle my pride whilst I lived. I had rather glide gently down the stream of life, leaving it to posterity to think and say what they please of me, than by any act of mine to have vanity or ostentation attributed to me. . . . I do not think vanity is a trait of my character.[8]

> He could still find time for a little rest and recreation in writing facetious letters to friends, such as William Gordon, underscoring for the clergyman sexual puns about old comrade Joseph Ward, who at age forty-nine took a bride.

I will not ascribe the intrepidity of his late enterprize to a mere *flash* of desires, because, in his military career he would have learnt how to distinguish between false alarms and a serious movement. Charity therefore induces me to suppose that like a prudent general, he had reviewed his *strength*, his arms, and ammunition before he got involved in an action—But if these have been neglected, and he has been precipitated into the measure, let me advise him to make the *first* onset upon his fair [Dulcinea] del Tobosa, with vigor, that the impression may be deep, if it cannot be lasting, or frequently renewed.[9]

> He likewise could joke about his serious experiment in breeding jackasses. In the spring of 1786, King Charles III of Spain had sent him a jack called "Royal Gift" that did not live up to expectations.

Though young, he follows what one may suppose to be the example of his late Royal Master, who cannot, tho' past his grand climacterick, perform seldomer, or with more Majestic solemnity, than he does. However I am not without hope that when he becomes a little better acquainted with republican enjoyments, he will amend his manners, and fall into a better and more expeditious mode of doing business.[10]

> He could also laugh at himself in the role of artist's model in demand for portraits and busts. Washington modeled for only about fifty of the five hundred portraits by contemporary artists.[11] Celebrated painter Gilbert Stuart said, "Washington's face is my fortune," having made sixty copies of the well known Athenaeum portrait, but he considered Houdon's bust the only accurate image.[12] Washington considered either medium an occupational hazard.

In for a penny, in for a pound is an old adage. I am so hackneyed to the touches of the Painters pencil, that I am *now* altogether at their beck, & set like Patience on a monument whilst they are delineating the lines of my face—It is a proof among many others of what habit and custom can effect—At first I was as impatient at the request, and as restive under the operation, as a Colt is of the Saddle—The next time, I submitted very reluctantly but with less flouncing—Now, no dray moves more readily to the Thill than I do to the Painters Chair.[13]

Sitting for sculpture took an even more painful toll. A mark of his fame was the decision by the great French sculptor Jean Antoine Houdon to cancel a commission from Catherine the Great in order to make a sculpture of Washington. At first he tried to work from a portrait by Charles Willson Peale and a bust by Joseph Wright—a bust that allegedly frightened Martha Washington.

[Wright came to Mount Vernon with the singular request, that I should permit him to take a model of my face, in plaster of Paris, to which I consented, with some reluctance. He oiled my features over; and placing me flat upon my back, upon a cot, proceeded to daub my face with the plaster. Whilst in this ludicrous attitude, Mrs. Washington entered the room; and seeing my face thus overspread with the plaster, involuntarily exclaimed. Her cry excited in me a disposition to smile, which gave my mouth a slight twist, or compression of the lips, that is now observable in the busts which Wright afterward made.][14]

In October 1785, when neither the bust nor the portrait suited Houdon, he came to Mount Vernon and subjected Washington to more plaster. However, his assistant dropped the cast, breaking it into a thousand pieces. Houdon started to do it again but Washington protested, for nothing in the world would he submit a second time.[15]

I have only to observe that not having a sufficient knowledge in the art of sculpture to oppose my judgment to the taste of Connoisseiurs, I do not desire to dictate in the matter—on the contrary I shall be perfectly satisfied with whatever may be judged decent and proper. I should even scarcely have ventured to suggest that perhaps a servile adherence to the garb of antiquity might not be altogether so expedient as some little deviation in favor of the modern custom [of contemporary dress].[16]

> Well aware of having to project a properly democratic image, with proper modesty he turned down Houdon's wish to pose him semi-naked in a classical toga. Instead he sent one of his uniforms to Paris for Gouverneur Morris, then on a mission to France, to model for the well-known statue of Washington shedding his sword for a ploughshare.
>
> As the Friend of the People, wherever Washington traveled crowds followed. On an extended tour of western lands, back-country fetes got in the way of his inspecting properties and potential routes from the Potomac River to the Ohio River. Revisiting scenes of exploits thirty years earlier—now stripped of nostalgia—received scant mention in his journal.

4th [October 1784]: I arrived at Colchester, 30 Miles, to Dinner; and reached home before Sun down; having travelled on the same horses since the first day of September by the computed distances 680 Miles. And tho' I was disappointed in one of the objects which induced me to undertake this journey namely to examine into the situation quality and advantages of the Land which I hold upon the Ohio and Great Kanhawa and to take measures for rescuing them from the hands of Land Jobbers and Speculators—who I had been informed regardless of my legal and equitable rights, Patents, etc; had enclosed them within other Surveys and were offering them for Sale at Philadelphia and in Europe. I say notwithstanding this disappointment, I am well pleased with my journey, as it has been the means of my obtaining a knowledge of facts—coming at the temper and disposition of the Western Inhabitants and making reflections thereon, which, otherwise, must have been as wild, incoherent, and perhaps as foreign from the

truth, as the inconsistencys of the reports which I had received even from those to whom most credit seemed due,
generally were.

These reflections remain to be summed up. The more
then the Navigation of Potomack is investigated, and duely
considered, the greater the advantages arising from them
appear.[17]

> In token of his service in the war, the Virginia legislature
> awarded him fifty shares of the Potomac Company, which
> was formed to open navigation to the Ohio. He accepted
> the first company presidency pro bono. He took the office
> seriously enough to explore the river personally. En route,
> at Frederick, Maryland, he could at last put business
> before the pleasure of being feted.

5th [August 1785]. In the Evening the Bells rang, and
Guns were fired; and a Committee waited upon me by order of the Gentlemen of the Town to request that I would
stay next day and partake of a public dinner which the Town
were desirous of giving me. But as arrangements had been
made, and the time for examining the Shannondoah Falls
. . . was short I found it most expedient to decline the
honor.[18]

> After much soul-searching, he turned down appeals to use
> his public influence in support of abolition, though he
> supported it in principle.

The unfortunate condition of the persons, whose labour
in part I employed, has been the unavoidable subject of
regret. To make the Adults among them as easy and as com-
fortable in their circumstances as their actual state of ignorance and improvidence would admit; and to lay a
foundation to prepare the rising generation for a destiny
different from that in which they were born; afforded some

satisfaction to my mind, and could not I hoped be displeasing to the justice of the Creator.[19]

There is not a man living who wishes more sincerely than I do, to see a plan adopted for the abolition of it—but there is only one proper and effectual mode by which it can be accomplished, and that is by Legislative authority: and this, as far as my suffrage will go, shall never be wanting.[20]

A similar conflict of principle and inclination arose when he was made president of the Society of the Cincinnati. This elite society was formed to bond and aid American officers and their families, and later expanded to included French officers. The mere formation, much less Washington's titular leadership, enraged democrats. They claimed the society aimed to form a new aristocracy.

Washington saw their point and tried to withdraw. When Jefferson recommended revising the society's charter, Washington replied, *"No! not a fibre of it must be retained—no half-way reformation will suffice. If the thing be bad, it must be totally abolished."*[21]

At its first meeting in Philadelphia in May 1784, he failed to abolish the Society. He accepted revisions, however, and remained the society's president to satisfy his old comrades and avert public turmoil.

It is a matter of little moment whether the alarm which siezed the public mind was the result of foresight—envy and jealousy—or a disordered imagination; the affect of perseverance would have been the same: wherein then would have been found an equivalent for the seperation of Interests, which (from my best information, not from one State only but many) would inevitably have taken place?[22]

Washington managed a tenuous balance of public and private interests. As president of the Potomac Company he was instrumental in bringing the states together. He called a conference at Mount Vernon (in March 1785) aimed at defining rights and responsibilities of Virginia and Maryland respecting Potomac navigation. This meeting led to better known Annapolis and Constitutional conventions. The members recommended that the two states meet every year. That winter, the Virginia legislature passed a resolution that *all* the states meet every year, a motion that Washington, though not in the legislature, actively supported.

When only five states sent delegates to convene at Annapolis (September 1786) he blamed his wartime nemesis, the Confederation, for the too-loose form of government.

Busy as he was with manifold private concerns, he was too sick and tired of national weakness to sit idly by. At the same time, he who had always striven to succeed was now unsure of success.

We have errors to correct. We have probably had too good an opinion of human nature in forming our confederation. Experience has taught us, that men will not adopt and carry into execution, measures the best calculated for their own good without the intervention of a coercive power. . . . We must take human nature as we find it. Perfection falls not to the share of mortals. . . . Retired as I am from the world, I frankly acknowledge I cannot feel myself an unconcerned spectator. Yet having happily assisted in bringing the ship into port and having been fairly discharged; it is not my business to embark again on a sea of troubles. Nor could it be expected that my sentiments and opinions would have much weight on the minds of my Countrymen—they have been neglected, tho' given as a last legacy in the most solemn manner. I had then perhaps some claims to public attention. I consider myself as having none at present.[23]

> Political weakness shared blame with human weakness. He
> saw its consequences in riots in Rhode Island and Massa-
> chusetts where Daniel Shays and followers seized the
> federal arsenal at Springfield.

The accounts which are published, of the commotions and temper of numerous bodies in the Eastern States, are equally to be lamented and deprecated. They exhibit a melancholy proof of what our trans atlantic foe have predicted; and of another thing perhaps, which is still more to be regretted, and is yet more unaccountable; that mankind left to themselves are unfit for their own government.

I am mortified beyond expression whenever I view the clouds which have spread over the brightest morn that ever dawned upon any Country. In a word, I am lost in amazement, when I behold what intriegueing; the interested views of desperate characters; Jealousy; and ignorance of the Minor part, are capable of effecting as a scourge on the major part of our fellow citizens of the Union: for it is hardly to be imagined that the great body of the people tho' they will not act can be so enveloped in darkness, or short sighted as not to see the rays of a distant sun through all this mist of intoxication and folly.[24]

> Despite recurring rheumatism in his shoulder and having
> vowed not to appear again on the public stage, Washing-
> ton reluctantly joined Virginia's delegation to the federal
> convention called for Philadelphia in May 1787.

After I had rendered an account on my military trust to congress and retired to my farm, I flattered myself that this unenviable lot was reserved for my latter years. . . . But in this I was disappointed. The Legislature of Virginia in opposition to my express desire signified in the clearest terms to the Governor of the State, appointed me a Delegate to the federal Convention. Never was my embarrassment or hesitation more extreme or distressing. By letters from some of the wisest and best men in almost every quarter of the Continent, I was advised, that it was my indispensable duty to attend, and that, in the deplorable condition to which our affairs were reduced, my refusal would be considered a desertion. . . . [25]

The pressure of the public voice was so loud, I could not resist the call to a convention of the States which is to determine whether we are to have a Government of respectability under which life—liberty, and property secured to us, or whether we are to submit to one which may be the result of chance or the moment, springing perhaps from anarch Confusion, and dictated perhaps by some aspiring demagogue who will not consult the interest of his Country so much as his own ambitious views.[26]

8

BECOMING PRESIDENT

1787–1789

As a delegate to the Philadelphia Convention, no one
could match Washington in background, experience, or
heroic personality. At twenty-three, the highest ranking
American officer; in his late thirties, a legislator leading
opposition to British policy; in his forties, the commander-
in-chief of American forces; in his early fifties, an activist
in opening the West; and now, in his late fifties, a living
symbol of classical and Christian magnanimity.

He entered Philadelphia escorted by the city's troops,
heralded by bells. Crowds would follow on fishing trips
and visits to Valley Forge. As soon as a quorum assembled
at the Convention, he was unanimously elected to preside.
As delegates were sworn to secrecy, he could not report
proceedings, but he kept up a running correspondence
with Mount Vernon on farm matters along with a diary of
extraconvention activities, including visits to local farms,
friends, and points of interest.

• Attendance in Convention—morning business, receiving, and returning visits—and Dining late with the
numberless etc—which are not avoided in so large a City
as Philadelphia.[1]

- General Washington presents his respectful compliments to Mrs Powell, and would, with great pleasure, have made one of a party for the *School for Scandall* this evening; had not every thing been arranged, and Mr Gouverneur Morris and himself on the point of stepping into the Carriage for a fishing expedition ... The General can but regret that matters have turned out so unluckily, after waiting so long to receive a lesson in the School for Scandal.[2]
- *Tuesday 31st [July].* Whilst Mr. Morris was fishing I rid over the old Cantonment of the American [army] of the Winter 1777 and 8. Visited all the Works, which were in Ruins; and the Incampments in woods where the ground had not been cultivated.
- On my return back to Mrs. [Jane] Moore's, observing some Farmers at Work, and entering into Conversation with them, I received the following information with respect to the mode of cultivating Buck Wheat, and the application of the grain. ...[3]
- *Monday 3d [September].* In Convention. Visited a Machine at Doctor Franklins (called a mangle) for pressing, in place of Ironing, clothes from the wash. Which Machine from the facility with which it dispatches business is well calculated for Table cloths & such Articles as have not pleats & irregular foldings and would be very useful in all large families. Dined, drank Tea, & spent the evening at Mr. Morris's.[4]

Much of the Convention's work was done in committees, but Washington's presence gave dignity and seriousness of purpose to the proceedings. Legends talk about the power of his mere stare to freeze familiarity or discipline carelessness—as when some delegate dropped a copy of minutes supposed to have been secret. William Pierce of Georgia said that Washington kept the paper until time to adjourn.

[I am sorry to find that some one member of this Body, has been so neglectful of the secrets of the Convention as to drop a copy of their proceedings. . . . I must entreat Gentlemen to be more careful, lest our transactions get into the News Papers and disturb the public repose by premature speculations. I know not whose Paper it is, but there it is (throwing it down on the table), let him who owns it take it.][5] (No one dared.)

• *Monday 17th [September]*. Met in Convention when the Constitution received the Unanimous assent of 11 States and Colonel Hamilton's from New York (the only delegates from thence in Convention) and was subscribed to by every Member present except Governor Randolph and Colonel Mason from Virginia and Mr. Gerry from Massachusetts. The business being thus closed, the Members adjourned to the City Tavern, dined together and took a cordial leave of each other—after which I returned to my lodgings—did some business with, and received the papers from the secretary of the Convention [William Jackson], and retired to meditate on the momentous work which had been executed, after not less than five, for a large part of the time Six, and sometimes 7 hours sitting every day, sundays and the ten days adjournment to give a Committee opportunity and time to arrange the business for more than four Months.[6]

He had earned a rest, having by force of personality alone, presided over a new birth of compromise. He spoke only once. On the last day, seemingly impatient to avoid debate on raising representatives per citizen from thirty to forty thousand, he announced his support and consequent influence because, *"He thought this of so much consequence that it would give him much satisfaction to see it adopted."*[7]

The various and opposite interests which were to be conciliated. The local prejudices which were to be subdued.

89

The diversity of opinions and sentiments which were to be reconciled. And in fine, the sacrafices which were necessary to be made on all sides, for the general welfare, combined to make it a work of so intricate and difficult a nature, that I think it is much to be wondered at, that any thing could have been produced with such unanimity as the Constitution proposed.[8]

> After four months and fourteen days, he was so anxious to get home to Mount Vernon that he risked his life and two horses in a foolhardy dash across a rotten bridge. He escaped harm, thanks to Providence, this time with the help of strangers.

Wednesday 19th. The rain which had fallen the preceeding evening having swelled the Water considerably there was no fording it safely. I was reduced to the necessity therefore of remaining on the other side or of attempting to cross an old, rotten and long disused bridge. Being anxious to get on I preferred the latter and in the attempt one of my horses fell 15 feet at least, the other very near following which (had it happened) would have taken the Carriage with baggage along with him and destroyed the whole effectually. However, by prompt assistance of some people at a Mill just by and great exertion, the first horse was disengaged from his harness, the second prevented from going quite through and drawn off and the Carriage rescued from hurt.[9]

> Reforming the government was not over yet. The Convention had recommended that the Constitution be ratified by conventions in at least nine states. At Virginia's convention, such formidable opponents as Patrick Henry and George Mason objected to the lack of a Bill of Rights. Washington was not at the state convention, but fearing

their great persuasive powers, he lobbied vigorously person-to-person. He met their objection by explaining that the Constitution made allowance for the omission of a Bill of Rights to be corrected by amendment.

I wish the Constitution which is offered had been made more perfect, but I sincerely believe it is the best that could be obtained at this time—and as a constitutional door is opened for amendments hereafter—the adoption of it under present circumstances of the Union is in my opinion desirable.[10]

To his great relief, Virginians ratified the Constitution on 25 June 1788 by ten hard-won votes. He shared the views of James Madison, who had led the fight in the state convention and would introduce the Bill of Rights in Congress.

The great danger, in my view, was that every thing might have been thrown into the last stage of Confusion before any government whatsoever could have been established; and that we should have suffered a political shipwreck, without the aid of one friendly star to guide us into Port. Every real patriot must have lamented that private feuds and local politics should have unhappily insinuated themselves into, and in some measure obstructed the discussion of a great national question. A just opinion, that the People when rightly informed will decide in a proper manner, ought certainly to have prevented all intemperate or precipitate proceedings on a subject of so much magnitude.

Nor should a regard to common decency have suffered the Zealots in the minority to have stigmatized the authors of the Constitution as Conspirators and Traitors. However unfavorably individuals, blinded by passion and prejudice, might have thought of the characters which composed the

[Federal] Convention; the election of those characters by the Legislatures of the several States and the reference of their Proceedings to the free determination of their Constituents, did not carry the appearance of *a private combination to destroy the liberties of their Country.* . . .

Newspapers had reported that Washington and Franklin were being misled by radicals to support the Constitution, characterizing Franklin as "a fool from age" and Washington as "a fool from nature."[11] He took such attacks on his integrity seriously.

For myself, I expected not to be exempted from obloquy any more than others. It is the lot of humanity. But if the shafts of malice had been aimed at me in ever so pointed a manner, on this occasion, involved as I was in a consciousness of having acted in conformity to what I believed my duty, they would have fallen blunted from their mark.

It is known to some of my countrymen and can be demonstrated to the conviction of all, that I was in a manner constrained to attend the general Convention in compliance with the earnest and pressing desires of many of the most respectable characters in different parts of the Continent.

At my age, and in my circumstances, what sinister object, or personal emolument had I to seek after, in this life? The growing infirmities of age and the encreasing love of retirement, daily confirm my decided predilection for domestic life: and the great searcher of human hearts is my witness, that I have no wish which aspires beyond the humble and happy lot of living and dying a private citizen on my own farm.[12]

Delegate Pierce Butler said it was no secret that the Convention had Washington in mind when they designed the presidency,[13] and the press assumed that he would be the first President. Washington had no comment in public but did confide his reluctance in private.

I must reserve to my self the right of making up my final decision, at the last moment when it can be no longer postponed; when all the circumstances can be brought into one view, & when the expediency and inexpediency of a *refusal* can be more judiciously determined than at present. . . . If from any inducement I shall be persuaded ultimately to accept it, it will not be (so far as I know my own heart) from any of a private or personal nature.

Every personal consideration conspires to rivet me (if I may use the expression) to retirement. At my time of life and under my circumstances, nothing in this world can ever draw me from it, unless it be a *conviction* that the partiality of my Countrymen had made my services absolutely necessary, joined to a *fear* that my refusal might induce a belief that I prefered the conservation of my own reputation and private ease to the good of my Country.

After all, if I should conceive my self in a manner constrained to accept, I call Heaven to witness, that this very act would be the greatest sacrafice of my personal feelings and wishes that ever I have been called upon to make. It would be to fore go repose and domestic enjoyment; for trouble, perhaps; for public obloquy: for I should consider myself as entering upon an unexplored field, enveloped on every side with clouds and darkness.

From this embarrassing situation, I had naturally supposed that my declarations at the close of the War would have saved me; and that my sincere intentions, then publicly made known, would have effectually precluded me for ever afterwards from being looked upon as a candidate for any Office. This hope, as a last anchor of worldly happiness in old age, I had still carefully preserved; untill the public papers and private letters from my Corrispondents in almost every quarter, taught me to apprehend that I might soon be obliged to answer the question, whether I would go again into public, or not?[14]

By March 1788 he had sought relief in diurnal routine as described by his secretary Tobias Lear.

[He rises every day before the sun—writes till breakfast (which never exceeds half past seven) then mounts his horse, and rides around his farm till half past two, sees that everything is in proper order—and if there is no company he writes till dark, and in the evening plays a game of whist.][15]

During the calm before the inevitable election, he kept busy managing his various properties and looking after the extended family. He had sent his late brother Sam's two mischievous sons, George and Lawrence, to Alexandria Academy. They were incorrigible scamps until Washington intervened with a stern lecture about habits of industry, economy, frugality, keeping only the best company, dressing neatly, and paying close attention to schoolwork.

If you comply with the advise herein given to pay a diligent attention to your studies, and employ your time of relaxation in proper company, you will find but few opportunities and little inclination, while you continue at an Academy, to enter into those scenes of vice and dissipation which too often present themselves to youth in every place, and particularly in towns. If you are determined to neglect your books, and plunge into extravagance and dissipation nothing I could now say would prevent it—for you must be employed, and if it is not in pursuit of those things which are profitable it must be in pursuit of those which are destructive.[16]

94

With the press predicting his unanimous election, Washington nevertheless remained in denial as late as Christmas time 1788, reiterating a heartfelt refrain.

My heartfelt wishes, and I would fain hope, the circumstances are opposed to it. I flatter myself my countrymen are so fully persuaded of my desire to remain in private life, that I am not without hopes and expectations of being left quietly to enjoy the repose, in which I am at present. . . . The great Searcher of human hearts knows there is no wish in mine, beyond that of living and dying an honest man, on my own farm.[17]

Known and unknown office seekers anticipating his election aggravated "a heart filled with distress, the ten thousand embarrassments, perplexities and troubles to which I must again be exposed in the evening of life, already near consumed in public cares . . ." and forced him to make plans contingent on human error.

I clearly foresaw the endless jealousies, and, possibly, the fatal consequences, to which a government, depending altogether on the good will of the people for its establishment, would certainly be exposed in its early stages. Besides, I thought, whatever the effect might be in pleasing or displeasing any individuals at the present moment, a due concern for my own reputation not less decisively than a sacred regard to the interests of the Community, required that I should hold myself absolutely at liberty to act, while in office, with a sole reference to justice and the public good. It is true, in such a fallible state of existence and from the want of a competent knowledge of character I may err: but my errors in my nominations shall be such as result from the head—and not from the heart.[18]

Unanimously named by electors, his inauguration would

not be official until Congresses quorum on 1 April 1789. To his intimate friend, Henry Knox, he confided his real sense of insecurity.

The delay may be compared to a reprieve; for in confidence I can assure *you*—with the *world* it would obtain *little credit*—that my movements to the chair of Government will be accompanied with feelings not unlike those of a culprit who is going to the place of his execution: so unwilling am I, in the evening of a life nearly consumed in public cares, to quit a peaceful abode for an Ocean of difficulties, without that competency of political skill—abilities and inclination which is necessary to manage the helm. I am sensible, that I am embarking the voice of the people and a good name of my own, on this voyage, but what returns will be made for them—Heaven alone can foretell.[19]

But by the end of January 1789, he had already formulated a sort of contingent mission statement.

My endeavours shall be unremittingly exerted (even at the hazard of former fame or present popularity) to extricate my country from the embarrassments in which it is entangled, through want of credit; and to establish, a general system of policy, which, if pursued will insure permanent felicity to the Commonwealth. I think I see a *path*, as clear and as direct as a ray of light, which leads to the attainment of that object. Nothing but harmony, honesty, industry and frugality are necessary to make us a great and happy people.[20]

Despite his own honesty, industry, and frugality, however, he was so cash poor that he put up his Ohio Valley property for sale or rent. Worse, when the official call finally came, Washington had to borrow from local merchant Richard Conway 625 pounds at 6 percent to pay his way to the capital.[21] Still, he retained the valuable capacity of not taking himself too seriously, as in thanking composer Francis Hopkinson for dedicating a book of music to him.

The Poets of old (whatever they may do in these days) were strangely addicted to the marvellous; and if I before *doubted* the truth of their relations with respect to the power of musick, I am now fully convinced of their falsity—because I would not, for the honor of my Country, allow that we are left by the Ancients at an *immeasurable* distance in everything; and if they could sooth the ferocity of wild beasts—could draw the trees and the stones after them—and could even charm the powers of Hell by their musick, I am sure that your productions would have had at least virtue enough in them (without the aid of voice or instrument) to soften the Ice of the Delaware and Potomack. . . .

Should the tide of prejudice not flow in favor of [the book] (and so various are the tastes, opinions and whims of men, that even the sanction of Divinity does not ensure universal concurrence) what, alass! can I do to support it? I can neither sing one of the songs, nor raise a single note on any instrument to convince the unbelieving.[22]

If he did not take himself seriously in that instance, he took the office of president so seriously as to depart from Mount Vernon in self-doubt bordering on despair.

[16 April 1789.] About ten o'clock I bade adieu to Mount Vernon, to private life, and to domestic felicity; and with a mind oppressed with more anxious and painful sensations than I have words to express, set out for New York. . . with the best dispositions to render service to my country in obedience to its call, but with less hope of answering its expectations.[23]

9

CREATING THE PRESIDENCY

1789–1793

Washington left Mount Vernon in good hands. Martha Washington's favorite niece Fanny Bassett, who had lived with them as their own child, had married Major George Washington, the son of the general's brother Charles and, since 1785, the manager of the estate. Following her husbands death from tuberculosis, Fanny proved a highly creditable successor in managing Mount Vernon. But when she asked the general's advice about remarrying, Martha Washington sadly replied for him, "The President never has, nor never will, as you have often heard him say, inter meddle in matrimonial concerns."[1] He did have confidence in her stewardship—except when she wasted fine wine on merely casual visitors.

Since I left Mount Vernon she has given out four dozen and eight bottles of wine. Whether they are used or not she does not say; but I am led by it to observe, that it is not my intention that it should be given to every one who may incline to make a convenience of the house in travelling; or who may be induced to visit it from motives of curiosity. . . . The duty upon Madeira wine makes it one of the most expensive liquors that is now used; while my stock of it is small and old wine (of which that is) is not to be had upon any terms for which reason ... I had rather you would provide Claret, or other wine on which the duty is not so high than to use my Madeira unless it be on extraordinary occasions.[2]

He left Martha Washington and her grandchildren to follow in May. His triumphal journey to New York by coach-and-four took a week, delayed by ceremonial receptions, formal escorts, and welcoming and acceptance speeches at every town. His farewell speech to neighbors in Alexandria prefigured Lincoln's farewell to his Springfield neighbors.

Those who have known me best (and you, my fellow citizens, are from your situation, in that number) know better than any others my love of retirement is so great, that no earthly consideration, short of a conviction of duty, could have prevailed upon me to depart from my resolution, "never more to take any share in transactions of a public nature." The whole tenor of my life has been open to your inspection; and my past actions, rather than my present declarations, must be the pledge of my future conduct. . . .

All that now remains for me is to commit myself and you to the protection of that beneficent Being, who on a former occasion hath happily brought us together, after a long and distressing separation—Perhaps the same gracious Providence will again indulge us with the same heartfelt felicity. But words, my fellow-citizens, fail me: *Unutterable sensations must then be left to more expressive silence: while, from an aching heart, I bid you all, my affectionate friends, and kind neighbours, farewell!*[3]

Baltimore and Wilmington feted him fit for a king. Then, as he crossed into Pennsylvania at Gray's Ferry, a cavalry of Philadelphians brought him a white horse to ride into town. He rode across a bridge festooned with bright flowers as little Angelica Peale suspended from above held a heroic wreath of laurel over his head. At Trenton a women's chorus hymned him through an arch of flowers as thirteen little girls spread blossoms in his path.[4]

A committee from Congress escorted him across Newark Bay on a new forty-seven-foot barge rowed by thirteen pilots. A flotilla of well-wishers and a school of porpoises followed in their wake. Beneath the glitter lingered niggling self-doubt.

[23 April 1789.] The display of boats which attended and joined us on this occasion, some with vocal and some with instrumental music on board; the decorations of the ships, the roar of cannon, and the loud acclamations of the people which rent the skies, as I passed along the wharves, filled my mind with sensations as painful (considering the reverse of this scene, which may be the case after all my labors to do good) as they are pleasing.[5]

He disembarked on a crimson carpet and, as a military escort stepped forward, he told their captain he would accept them this time but in future would rely for protection on the affection of "my fellow-citizens."

With no precedent, the inauguration followed the model of the coronation of George the Third—except that the King had ridden a white horse into Westminster Abbey. (During periods of mental illness George hallucinated that he himself was General Washington.[6]) Not a majestic speaker under any circumstances, Washington appeared to New York Senator William Maclay "agitated and embarrassed more than ever he was by the leveled Cannon or pointed Musket. . . ."

[He trembled, and several times could scarce make out to read, tho it must be supposed he had often read it before. He put part of the fingers of his left hand, into the side, of what I think the Taylors call the fall, of his Breetches. Changing the paper into his left hand, after some time, he then did the same with some fingers of his right hand. When he came to the Words all the world, he made a flourish with his right hand, which left rather an ungainly impression. I sincerely, for my part, wished all set ceremony in the hands of the dancing Masters, and that this first of Men, had read off, his address, in the plainest Manner without ever taking his Eyes From the paper. . . . He was dressed in deep brown, with Metal buttons, with an Eagle on them, White stockings a Bag and Sword.][7]

Maclay guessed correctly that Washington had worked on the speech many times. Summarizing how he felt about losing private life for public service, many passages could have been taken as a surfeit of self-pity, and so he deleted them.

I solemnly assert and appeal to the searcher of hearts to witness the truth of it, that my leaving home to take upon myself the execution of this Office was the greatest personal sacrifice I have ever, in the course of my existence, been called upon to make.

Although when the last war had become inevitable, I heartily concurred in the measures taken by my country for repelling force by force; yet it is known, I was so far from aspiring to the chief Military command, that I accepted it with unfeigned reluctance. My fellow-soldiers of the late patriotic Army will bear me testimony that when I accepted that appointment, it was not to revel in luxury, to grow proud of rank, to eat the bread of idleness, to be insensible to the sufferings, or to refuse a share in the toils and dangers to which they were exposed.

I need not say what were the complicated cares, the cruel reverses or the unusual perplexities inseparable from my office, to prove that I have prematurely grown old in the Service of my Country. For in truth, I have now arrived at that sober age, when, aside of any extraordinary circumstances to deter me from encountering new fatiegues, and when, without having met with any particular shocks to injure the constitution, the love of retirement naturally encreases. . . .

After I had rendered an account of my military trust to congress and retired to my farm, I flattered myself that this unenviable lot was reserved for my latter years. I was delighted with agricultural affairs and excepting a few avocations [contented] myself with the idea it was all that would ever be expected at my hand. But in this I was disappointed. The Legislature of Virginia in opposition to my express desire signified in the clearest terms to the Governor of that State, appointed me a Delegate to the federal Convention. Never was my embarrassment or hesitation more extreme or distressing. By letters from some of the wisest and best men in almost every quarter of the Continent, I was advised, that it was my indispensable duty to attend, and that, in the deplorable condition to which our affairs were reduced, my refusal would be considered a desertion of [duty]. . . .

Neither life or reputation has been accounted dear in my sight. And, from the bottom of my Soul, I know, that my motives on no former occasion were more innocent than in the present instance. At my time of life and in my situation I will not suppose that many moments need be bestowed in exculpating myself from any suggestions, which might be made that the incitement of pleasure or grandeur, or power have wrought a change in my resolution. . . .

If I have formerly served the community without a wish for pecuniary compensation, it can hardly be suspected that I am at present influenced by avaricious schemes. In the next place, it will be recollected, that the Divine Providence hath not seen fit, that my blood should be transmitted or my name perpetuated by the endearing, though sometimes seducing channel of immediate offspring. I have no child for whom I could wish to make a provision—no family to build in greatness upon my Country's ruins. . . . Let my personal enemies if I am so unfortunate as to have deserved such a return from any one of my countrymen, point to the sinester object, or to the earthly consideration beyond the hope of rendering some little service to our parent Country, that could have persuaded me to accept this appointment. . . .

Thus I have explained the general impressions under which I have acted: omitting to mention untill the last, a principal reason which induced my acceptance. After a consciousness that all is right within and an humble hope of approbation in Heaven—nothing can, assuredly, be so grateful to a virtuous man as the good opinion of his fellow citizens. Though the partiality of mine led them to consider my holding the Chief Magistracy as a matter of infinitely more consequence than it really is; yet my acceptance must be ascribed rather to an honest willingness to satisfy that partiality, than to an overweening presumption upon my own capacity. Whenever a government is to be instituted or changed by Consent of the people, confidence in the person placed at the head of it, is, perhaps, more peculiarly necessary.[8]

Washington sought advice and assistance in establishing

the office of chief executive for a democratic republic. Hamilton advised on policy, Madison on mechanics of governing, John Jay on foreign affairs until Jefferson returned from France. Washington, ever self-conscious about his writings, had employed aides in the military and secretaries at home. Now he had political advisors to draft public statements. Madison found himself composing Congress's welcoming address, as well as the president's response. Washington would not forget that everything he did set a precedent for the office of president and incumbents to come.

Many things which appear of little importance in themselves and at the beginning, may have great and durable consequences from their having been established at the commencement of a new general Government. It will be much easier to commence the administration, upon a well adjusted system built on tenable grounds, than to correct errors or alter inconveniences after they shall have been confirmed by habit. The President in all matters of business and etiquette, can have no object but to demean himself in his public character, in such a manner as to maintain the dignity of Office, without subjecting himself to the imputation of superciliousness or unnecessary reserve.[9]

He would hold receptions on Tuesdays and official dinners on Thursdays. He would put in an appearance at Mrs. Washington's receptions on Fridays, very careful to balance democratic openness with the monarchical reserve needed to protect him from a demanding public.

I was unable to attend to any business *whatsoever*; for Gentlemen, consulting their own convenience rather than mine, were calling from the time I rose from breakfast—often before—until I sat down to dinner—This, as I resolved not to neglect my public duties, reduced me to the choice of one of these alternatives, either to refuse them *altogether*, or to appropriate a time for the reception of them—The first would, I well knew, be disgusting to many—The latter, *I expected* would undergo animadversion, and blazoning from those who find fault, *with*, or *without* cause. To please every body was impossible—I therefore adopted that line of conduct which combined public advantage with private convenience, and which in my judgment was unexceptionable in itself.

That I have not been able to make bows to the taste of [everyone] . . . is to be regretted especially too as (upon those occasions) they were indiscriminately bestowed, and the best I was master of—would it not have been better to have thrown the veil of charity over them, ascribing their stiffness to the effects of age, or to the unskilfulness of my teacher, than to pride and dignity of office, which God knows has no charms for me?[10]

In relations with Congress, Washington's pride of office would prevail. He set precedent for consulting the Senate on treaties after, rather than before, they were made. In August 1789 having gone to the Senate in person seeking advice and consent to Indian treaties, he stalked out when the question was referred to committee ("This defeats every purpose of my coming here"). He returned next day but, receiving neither advice nor consent, stalked out again, never to return.

At the same time, although the Cabinet had been designed to provide advice only in their limited fields, Washington began meeting with them regularly (as if a general staff in the army) on all matters. Perhaps forgetting wartime squabbling among generals and politicians, he did not foresee inter-Cabinet rivalry creating a pandemonium of party politics in which all hell would break loose.

I have been taught to believe that there is, in most polished nations, a system established, with regard to the foreign as well as the other great Departments, which, from the utility, the necessity, and the reason of the thing, provides that business should be digested and prepared by the Heads of those Departments. The impossibility that one man should be able to perform all the great business of the State, I take to have been the reason for instituting the great Departments, and appointing officers therein, to assist the Supreme Magistrate in discharging the duties of his trust. And, perhaps I may be allowed to say of myself, that the Supreme Magistrate of no State can have a greater variety of important business to perform in person, than I have at this moment.[11]

> On 15 October 1789 he began a month's tour of New England "to acquire knowledge of the face of the Country, the growth and Agriculture there of and the temper and disposition of the Inhabitants towards the new government."[12] Besides taking his usual detailed notes on the land, people, and crops, he recorded a conflict of wills with Governor John Hancock over the proper respect to be shown the people's president.

Saturday 24th. Having engaged yesterday to take an informal dinner with the Governor today (but under a full persuasion that he would have waited upon me so soon as I should have arrived) I excused myself upon his not doing it, and informing me thro his Secretary that he was too much indisposed [from gout] to do it.

Sunday 25th. The Lieutenant Governor and two of the Council . . . were sent here last Night to express the

Governor's Concern that he had not been in a condition to call upon me so soon as I came to Town. I informed them in explicit terms that I should not see the Governor unless it was at my own lodgings. . . .

I received a visit from the Governor, who assured me that Indisposition alone had prevented his doing it yesterday, and that he was still indisposed; but as it had been suggested that he expected to *receive* the visit from the President, which he knew was improper, he was resolved at all hazards to pay his Compliments to day.[13]

> Despite the complaint that such tours savor "too much of monarchy,"[14] the following spring—from March to July 1791—he also toured the southern states. This time, he prepared as for a military campaign.

Having obtained before I left Philadelphia the most accurate account, I could get there, of the places and roads through, and by which I was to perform my tour; and the distances between the former; I formed my line of march accordingly; fixed each days journey and the day to halt; from neither of which have I departed in a single instance. . . . But the improbability of performing a tour of 1700 miles (—I have already rode more), with the same set of horses without encountering any accident by which a deviation would be rendered unavoidable appeared so great that I allowed eight days for casualties, and six to refresh. . . . [15]

> He interrupted the expedition to take care of business at Mount Vernon. Among the many details awaiting him, not least was raising his niece Harriot Washington. She was the orphaned child of his brother Sam and had lived at Mount Vernon since age thirteen. When she turned sixteen Uncle Washington took time from his busy schedule (30 October 1791) to tender advice.

Occupied as my time now is, and must be during the sitting of Congress, I nevertheless will endeavor to inculcate upon your mind the delicacy and danger of that period, to which you are now arrived under peculiar circumstances. You are just entering into the state of womanhood without the watchful eye of a Mother to admonish, or the protecting aid of a Father to advise and defend you; you may not be sensible that you are at this moment about to be stamped with that character which will adhere to you through life—the consequence of which you have not perhaps attended to, but be assured it is of utmost importance that you should. . . .

Think then to what dangers a giddy girl of 15 or 16 must be exposed in circumstances like these. To be under but little or no controul may be pleasing to a mind that does not reflect, but this pleasure cannot be of long duration, and reason, too late perhaps, may convince you of the folly of misspending time. You are . . . to learn, I am certain, that your fortune is small—supply the want of it then with a well cultivated mind, with dispositions to industry and frugality—with gentleness of manners—obliging temper—and such qualifications as will attract notice, and recommend you to a happy establishment for life.

You might instead of associating with those from whom you can derive nothing that is good, but may have observed every thing that is deceitful, lying, and bad, become the intimate companion of and aid to your Cousin [Fanny Bassett] in the domestic concerns of the family.

> Perhaps reminded of how he made his own way in the world, Washington went on to recommend "a steady and rigid attention to the rules of propriety."

Many Girls before they have arrived at your age have been found so trustworthy as to take the whole trouble of a family from their Mothers; but it is by a steady and rigid attention to the rules of propriety that such confidence is obtained, and nothing would give me more pleasure than to hear that you had acquired it. The merits and benefits of it would redound more to your own advantage in your progress thro' life, and to the person with whom you may in due time form a matrimonial connexion than to any others—but to none would such a circumstance afford more real satisfaction than to Your affectionate Uncle G. Washington.[16]

Continuing his tour of the South meant enduring the usual mix of human error and providential blessing along with the smothering adulation of a grateful public.

Thursday 7th April. Recommenced my journey with Horses apparently well refreshed and in good spirits. In attempting to cross the ferry at Colchester with the four Horses hitched to the Chariot by neglect of the person who stood before them, one of the leaders got overboard when the boat was in swimming water and 50 yards from the Shore—with much difficulty he escaped drowning before he could be disengaged.

His struggling frightned the others in such a manner that one after another and in quick succession they all got over board harnessed and fastened as they were and with the utmost difficulty they were saved and the Carriage escaped being dragged after them as the whole of it happened in swimming water and at a distance from the shore. Providentially—indeed miraculously—by the exertions of people who went off in Boats and jumped into the River as soon as the Batteau was forced into wading water—no damage was sustained by the Horses, Carriage or harness.

He also included comments best described as chuckling to himself.

Friday 15th. Having suffered very much by the dust yesterday and finding that parties of Horse, and a number of other Gentlemen were intending to attend me part of the way to day, I caused their enquiries respecting the time of my setting out, to be answered that, I should endeavor to do it before eight O'clock; but I did it a little after five, by which means I avoided the inconveniences above-mentioned.

Monday 18th. [Tarborough] is less than Hallifax, but more lively and thriving; it is situated on Tar River which goes into Pamplico Sound and is crossed at the Town by means of a bridge a great height from the Water and notwithstanding the freshes rise sometimes nearly to the arch. Corn, Porke and some Tar are the exports from it. We were received at this place by as good a salute as could be given with one piece of artillery.

Sunday 3d [July]. Received, and answered an address from the Inhabitants of York town [Pennsylvania]—and there being no Episcopal Minister in the place, I went to hear morning Service in the Dutch reformed Church—which being in Dutch not a word of which I understood I was in no danger of becoming a proselyte to it by the eloquence of the Preacher.[17]

> Notwithstanding clouds of southern discontent, Indian unrest on the frontiers, and an Anglo-French war, he found public morale so high that people attributed prosperity to his administration rather than Providence.

The Farmer—the Merchant—and the Mechanic have seen their several Interests attended to, and from thence they unite in placing a confidence in their representatives, as well as in those in whose hands the Execution of the Laws is placed. Industry has there taken place of idleness, and oeconomy of dissipation. Two or three years of good crops, and a ready market for the produce of their lands has put every one in good humour; and, in some instances they even impute to the Government what is due only to the goodness of Providence.

Moreover, the tour reassured him that Hamilton's financial planning had at last secured public credit at home and abroad.

The establishment of public credit, is an immense point gained in our national concerns. This, I believe, exceeds the expectation of the most sanguine among us, and a late instance, unparalleled in this Country, has been given of the confidence reposed in our measures, by the rapidity with which the subscriptions to the Bank of the United States were filled. In two hours after the Books were opened by the Commissioners the whole number of shares were taken up, and four thousand more applied for than were allowed by the Institution; besides a number of Subscriptions which were coming on. This circumstance was not only pleasing as it related to confidence in Government; but as it exhibited an unexpected proof of the resources of our Citizens.[18]

In private, however, he saw that Hamilton's schemes were splitting the Cabinet. The chief antagonists were unfortunately favorites of his. Pragmatist Hamilton, Secretary of Treasury, who had begun as a military aide and become like a son to Washington, now sought tight federal controls. Philosopher Jefferson, Secretary of State, wartime governor of Virginia and diplomat in France, insisted on restraints proper to a representative democracy. As feuding developed into Federalist and Democratic-Republican parties, Washington feared the inevitable consequences.

How unfortunate would it be, if a fabric so goodly—

erected under so many Providential circumstances—and in its first stages, having acquired such respectibility, should, from diversity of Sentiments, or internal obstructions to some of the acts of Government (for I cannot prevail on myself to believe that these measures are, as yet, the deliberate acts of a determined party) should be harrowing our vitals in such a manner as to have brought us to the verge of dissolution. Melancholy thought![19]

Jefferson compromised on Hamilton's funding scheme in exchange for locating the national capital in the District of Columbia. Otherwise their insidious feuding caused Washington "extreme wretchedness."[20] Despairing of compromise, he asked Madison in private (20 May 1792) to draft a farewell address before the fall election, willing to risk criticism for such an early declaration.

A previous declaration to retire, not only carries with it the appearance of vanity and self importance, but it may be construed into a Manoeuvre to be invited to remain. And on the other hand, to say nothing, implys consent; or at any rate, would leave the matter in doubt; and to decline afterwards might be deemed as bad, and uncandid. . . .

Among other topics, he asked Madison to urge more civil public discourse, especially in the press.

However necessary it may be to keep a watchful eye over public servants, and public measures, yet there ought to be limits to it; for suspicions unfounded, and jealousies too lively, are irritating to honest feelings; and oftentimes are productive of more evil than good.[21]

He always tried to restrain his own powerful feelings before the public. News of an Indian ambush that took nine hundred men arrived during Mrs. Washington's Friday afternoon reception. He restrained himself until

the guests had left, then cursed the commanding officer so
angrily he frightened the ladies of the house.[22] He could
not, however, long sustain calm in blasts from a partisan
press. He despaired of protecting a nation uniquely
blessed from damning itself to destruction.

I shall be happy ... to see a cessation of the abuses of
public Officers, and of those attacks upon almost every
measure of government with which some of the Gazettes
are so strongly impregnated; and which cannot fail, if per-
severed in with the malignancy they now teem, of rending
the Union asunder. The Seeds of discontent, distrust, and
irritations which are so plentifully sown, can scarcely fail
to produce this effect and Mar that prospect of happiness
which perhaps never beamed with more effulgence upon
any people under the Sun. . . . In a word if the Government
and the Officers of it are to be the constant theme for Newspaper abuse, and this too without condescending to investigate the motives or the facts, it will be impossible, I
conceive, for any man living to manage the helm, or to keep
the machine together.[23]

10

PRESERVING THE PRESIDENCY

1793–1797

In 1793, Jefferson and Hamilton teamed to persuade Washington that he was indispensable. With no opposition, his unanimous reelection led him to hope for domestic tranquillity. Downplaying ritual that would hint of monarchy, he stripped the second inauguration of ceremony. Problems of policy and people persisted while circumstances at home and abroad went beyond control.

At home, Hamilton had imposed heavy taxes on spirits—25 percent on a gallon of whiskey which sold for twenty-five cents. Overseas, war flared between Britain and France. The British seized American ships at sea and seamen. The French insisted that the United States honor the 1778 treaty promising to protect French interests. The madcap French envoy Edmond Genet stormed the states, stirring up support for the French Revolution. Indian tribes on the western frontier beat back repeated attempts to pacify them. Washington experienced no joy in reelection.

To say I feel pleasure from the prospect of *commencing* another tour of duty, would be a departure from truth; for however it might savour of affectation in the opinion of

---

the world (who by the bye can only guess at my sentiments as it never has been troubled with them) my particular and confidential friends well know, that it was after a long and painful conflict in my own breast, that I was withheld (by considerations which are not necessary to mention) from requesting, *in time,* that no vote might be thrown away upon me; it being my fixed determination to return to the walks of private life, at the end of my term.[1]

Respite and recreation were denied him. He was called back from vacation at Mount Vernon by outbreak of war in Europe.

My visit to Mount Vernon (intended to be short when I set out) was curtailed by the Declaration of War by France against Great Britain and Holland; for I foresaw in the moment information of that event came to me at that place the necessity for announcing the disposition of this Country towards the Belligerent Powers; and the propriety of restraining, as far as a Proclamation would do it, our citizens from taking part in the contest.[2]

On Hamilton's advice, Washington issued a proclamation declaring neutrality. Jefferson protested that he exceeded his authority. Jefferson's supporters took it as violating republican principles. Philip Freneau's *National Gazette* supported Jefferson. John Fenno's *Gazette of the United States* supported Hamilton. Attacks on the presidency were redirected to the president. Washington erupted in a 2 August 1793 meeting recorded by Jefferson.

[Knox in a foolish incoherent sort of a speech introduced the Pasquinade lately printed, called the funeral of George W—— and James W(ilso)n, king and judge etc. where the President was placed on a Guillotin. The President was much inflamed, got into one of those passions when he cannot

*command himself. Run on much on the personal abuse
which had been bestowed on him. Defied any man on earth
to produce one single act of his since he had been in the
government which was not done on the purest motives. That
he had never repented but once the having slipped the
moment of resigning his office, and that was every moment
since. That by god he had rather be in his grave than in his
present situation. That he had rather be on his farm than to
be made emperor of the world and yet that they were
charging him with wanting to be a king.]*[3]

Verbatim or not, Jefferson's notes captured the
president's feeling of futility.

*[Aug. 6, 1793. The President calls on me at my house in the
country, and introduces my letter of July 31 announcing that
I should resign at the close of the next month. He again
expressed his repentance at not having resigned himself, and
how much it was increased by seeing that he was to be
deserted by those on whose aid he had counted: that he did
not know where he should look to find characters to fill up
the offices. . . . He told me that Colonel Hamilton had 3 or 4
weeks ago written to him, informing him that private as well
as public reasons had brought him to the determination to
retire, and that he should do it towards the close of the next
session. . . .*

*He expressed great apprehensions at the fermentation
which seemed to be working in the minds of the public, that
many descriptions of persons, actuated by different causes
appeared to be uniting, what it would end in he knew not. . . .
And he concluded by desiring that I would take 2 or 3 days
to consider whether I could not stay in till the end of another
quarter, for that like a man going to the gallows he was
willing to put it off as long as he could: but if I persisted, he*

must then look about him and make up his mind to do the best he could: and so he took leave.][4]

At the close of 1793 Jefferson resigned, leaving the struggle to followers in the House of Representatives. Hamilton resigned a year later but continued to act as adviser to the President.

British raids on American shipping peaked at three hundred. Washington sent John Jay to negotiate some kind of peaceful settlement. Hamilton, after preparing Jay's instructions, leaked them to the British.[5] The resulting treaty favored Great Britain, feeding the Francophile frenzy of radical Democratic Societies and Jefferson's Republicans.

The president's shield of Olympian indifference was wearing wafer thin from repeated attacks in the *National Gazette* and Philadelphia's *Aurora* (which accused him of "pusillanimous conduct"[6]).

That there are in this, as well as in all other Countries, discontented characters, I well know; as also that these characters are actuated by very different views: Some good, from an opinion that the measures of the General Government are impure: some bad, and (if I might be allowed to use so harsh an expression) diabolical; inasmuch as they are not only meant to impede the measures of Government generally, but more especially (as a great mean towards the accomplishment of it) to destroy the confidence, which it is necessary for the people to place (until they have unequivocal proof of demerit) in their public servants; for in this light I consider myself, whilst I am an occupant of office; and, if they were to go further and call me their slave, (during this period) I would not dispute the point.

But in what will all this abuse terminate? The result, as it respects myself, I care not; for I have a consolation within, that no earthly efforts can deprive me of, and that is, that neither ambition nor interested motives have influenced my conduct. The arrows of malevolence, therefore, however barbed and well pointed, never can reach the most vulnerable part of me; though, whilst I am *up* as a *mark*, they will be continually aimed.[7]

> Rumors reached him that Jefferson had been attacking the president as favoring the British versus his old allies. Washington tried to assume a charitable stance, attributing the alleged remarks to Jefferson's irony. But the president had irony of his own.

There could not be the trace of doubt on [Jefferson's] mind of predilection in mine, towards G. Britain or her politics, unless (which I do not believe) he has set me down as one of the most deceitful, and uncandid men living; because, not only in private conversations between ourselves, on this subject; but in my meetings with the confidential servants of the public, he has heard me often, when occasions presented themselves, express very different sentiments with an energy that could not be mistaken by *any one* present.[8]

> Even old friends criticized him. When Edmund Pendleton disagreed with the president's lenient policy towards the Six Nations, Washington pointed out that they were subject to unfair conditions similar to his own as president and as owner of extensive lands in their regions.

They are not without serious causes of complaint, from the encroachments which are made on their lands by our people; who are not to be restrained by any law now in being, or likely to be enacted. They, poor wretches, have no Press thro' which their grievances are related; and it is well known, that when one side only of a Story is heard, and often repeated, the human mind becomes impressed with it, insensibly. . . . These people are very much irritated by the continual pressure of land speculators and settlers on one hand; and by the impositions of unauthorised, and unprincipled traders (who rob them in a manner of their hunting) on the other.[9]

Under such conditions and because he was too busy to tend them, he decided to sell his lands in western Pennsylvania, scene of his youthful military career.

Having from long experience found, that landed property at a distance from, the proprietor, who is not able to pay attention to it, is more productive of plague than profit, I feel strongly disposed to sell all the lands I hold on the Ohio and Great Kanawah. . . . They are the cream of the country in which they lye.[10]

Sales over five years brought an estimated fifty thousand dollars with no discernible nostalgia. Under considerable stress, he seems to have found plenty of time to counsel the young people of his extended family, as in this delightful response to his adored granddaughter, beautiful but spoiled, eighteen-year-old Nelly Custis. She had complained about the callow youths at the Georgetown ball, vowing "never to give herself a moment's uneasiness on account of any of them." Washington commiserated.

A hint here; men and women feel the same inclinations to each other *now* that they have always done, and which they will continue to do until there is a new order of things, and *you*, as others have done, may find, perhaps, that the passions of your sex are easier raised than allayed. Do not therefore boast too soon or too strongly of your insensibility to, or resistance of, its powers. In the composition of the human frame there is a good deal of inflammable matter, however dormant it may lie for a time, and like an intimate acquaintance of yours, when the torch is put to it, *that* which is *within you* may burst into a blaze; for which reason, and especially too, as I have entered upon the chapter of advices, I will read you a lecture drawn from this text.

Love is said to be an involuntary passion, and it is, therefore, contended that it can not be resisted. This is true in part only, for like all things else, when nourished and supplied plentifully with aliment, it is rapid in its progress; but let these be withdrawn and it may be stifled in its birth or much stinted in its growth. For example, a woman (the same may be said of the other sex) all beautiful and accomplished, will, while her hand and heart are undisposed of, turn the heads and set the circle in which she moves on fire. Let her marry, and what is the consequence. The madness *ceases* and all is quiet again. Why? not because there is any dimunition in the charms of the lady, but because there is an end of hope.

Hence it follows, that love may and therefore ought to be under the guidance of reason, for although we can not avoid first impressions, we may assuredly place them under guard; and my motives for treating on this subject are to show you, while you remain Eleanor Parke Custis, spinster, and retain the resolution to love with moderation, the propriety of adhering to the latter resolution, at least until you have secured your game, and the way by which it may be accomplished.[11]

> When her older sister Eliza was eighteen, he had sent a shorter lecture on love and marriage, tempting to apply to his own courtship thirty-five years earlier.

Do not ... in your contemplation of the marriage state, look for perfect felicity before you consent to wed. Nor conceive, from the fine tales the Poets and lovers of old have told us, of the transports of mutual love, that heaven has taken its abode on earth: Nor do not deceive yourself in supposing, that the only mean by which these are to be obtained, is to drink deep of the cup, and revel in an ocean of love.

Love is a mighty pretty thing; but like all other delicious things, it is cloying; and when the first transports of the passion begins to subside, which it assuredly will do, and yield—oftentimes too late—to more sober reflections, it serves to evince, that love is too dainty a food to live *alone*, and ought not to be considered farther than as a necessary ingredient for that matrimonial happiness which results from a combination of causes—none of which are of greater importance than that the object on whom it is placed, should possess good sense, good dispositions, and the means of supporting you in the way you have been brought up.

Such qualifications cannot fail to attract (after marriage) your esteem and regard, into which, or into disgust, sooner or later, love naturally resolves itself; and who at the same time, has a claim to the respect, and esteem of the circle he moves in. Without these, whatever may be your first impressions of the man, they will end in disappointment; for be assured, and experience will convince you, that there is no truth more certain than that all our enjoyments fall short of our expectations; and to none does it apply with more force, than to the gratification of the passions.[12]

Poor Eliza should have listened. She wed aristocratic Britisher Thomas Law on the expectation that he would introduce her at the royal court. Tiring of her pretensions, he moved to Vermont and divorced her.[13]

Washington declined to comment on his own love life in public. When neighbor Elizabeth Powel teased him that she had found in a desk drawer warm love letters he had sent to Mrs. Washington, he replied that their warmth was all in Mrs. Powel's imagination.[14]

He would not of course respond to absurd wartime British propaganda accusing him of sexual escapades, as when Rivington's *New York Gazette* printed the claim of Betsey Sidman who said Washington fathered her baby, "conceived at the tap-house of her uncle Slutt."[15]

To Nelly, he offered a practical guide to choosing a mate with due attention to propriety in balancing head and heart.

When the fire is beginning to kindle, and your heart growing warm, propound these questions to it.

- Who is the invader?
- Have I a competent knowledge of him?
- Is he a man of good character; a man of sense? For, be assured, a sensible woman can never be happy with a fool.
- What has been his walk of life?
- Is he a gambler, a spendthrift, or drunkard?
- Is his fortune sufficient to maintain me in the manner I have been accustomed to live, and my sisters do live?
- And is he one to whom my friends can have no reasonable objection?

If these interrogatories can be satisfactorily answered, there will remain but one more to be asked, that, however, is an important one.

- Have I sufficient ground to conclude that his affections are engaged by me?

Without this the heart of sensibility will struggle against a passion that is not reciprocated—delicacy, custom, or call it by whatever epithet you will, having precluded all advances on your part. The declaration, without the *most in-*

direct invitation of yours, must proceed from the man, to render it permanent and valuable, and nothing short of good sense and an easy unaffected conduct can draw the line between prudery and coquetry. It would be no great departure from truth to say, that it rarely happens otherwise than that a thorough-paced coquette dies in celibacy, as a punishment for her attempts to mislead others, by encouraging looks, word, or actions, given for no other purpose than to draw men on to make overtures that they may be rejected.[16]

> After such paternal recreation, he found little rest. In addition to problems in the Cabinet, he faced foes and woes foreign and domestic. In September of 1794, he had to call out state militias to put down the antitax mob in western Pennsylvania called the Whiskey rebels. In full dress uniform he rode with troops as far as Bedford, Pennsylvania. There he turned over command to Alexander Hamilton. Letting Hamilton—who had imposed the tax three years earlier—lead the troops was a sign that Washington's fear of disorder had suppressed his well-honed sense of public relations. Reaction to a uniformed president marching against his people was tempered by the people's filial attitude. In his diary, Washington considered the part he played in the Whiskey Rebellion as merely inspirational.

> *6th to the 12th.* Employed in Organizing the several detachments, which had come in from different Counties of this State, in a very disjointed and loose manner; or rather I ought to have said in urging and assisting [Governor Thomas] Mifflin to do it; as I no otherwise took the command of the Troops than to press them forward, and to provide them with necessaries for their March, as well, and as far, as our means would admit. . . .

As I considered the support of the Laws as an object of the first magnitude, and the greatest part of the expense had already been incurred, that nothing Short of the most unequivocal *proofs* of absolute Submission should retard the March of the army into the Western counties, in order to convince them that the government could, and would enforce obedience to the laws—not suffering them to be insulted with impunity....

18th [at Bedford]. It appears evident that the people in the Western Counties of this State have got very much alarmed at the approach of the Army; but though Submission is professed, their principles remain the same; and that nothing but coercion, and example will reclaim and bring them to a due and unequivocal submission to the Laws.[17]

Of the seventeen tried, two rioters were subsequently convicted. In November his annual message to Congress blamed the Democratic Societies ("certain self-created societies") of provoking their insurrection. This infuriated the swelling opposition party. Jefferson's followers were already angry at the administration's willingness to treat with old enemy Britain but not old friend France. Still, Washington tried holding his disintegrating Cabinet together.

I view the opposition which the treaty is receiving from the meetings in different parts of the Union in a very serious light. Not because there is *more* weight in *any* of the objections which are made to it, than were foreseen at first. ... Nor as it respects myself personally, for this shall have no influence on my conduct; plainly perceiving, and I am accordingly preparing my mind for, the obloquy which disappointment and malice are collecting to heap upon my character.

But I am alarmed on account of the effect it may have

on, and the advantage the French government may be disposed to make of, the spirit which is at work; to cherish a belief in them, that the treaty is calculated to favor Great Britain at their expence. Whether they believe, or disbelieve these tales, the effect it will have upon the nation, will be nearly the same. . . .

When they see the people of this Country divided, and such a violent opposition given to the measures of their own government, pretendedly in their favor, it may be extremely embarrassing, to say no more of it. To sum the whole up in a few words, I have never, since I have been in the Administration of the government, seen a crisis which, in my judgment, has been so pregnant of interesting events.[18]

> Virtually ignored in October 1795, a treaty with Spain gave the United States access to New Orleans and the Mississippi. But the press and public had more interest in scandal as Hamilton followers in the Cabinet—Oliver Wolcott Jr. and Timothy Pickering—conspired to falsely accuse Edmund Randolph, then secretary of state, of taking a bribe from the French to delay ratifying the Jay treaty. Randolph's resignation filled the Cabinet with Federalists.
>
> Randolph promptly published a pamphlet vindicating himself and implying the president was a co-conspirator. Washington composed an irate reply, suppressing anguish at Randolph's alleged betrayal—another Benedict Arnold—and anger at his having publicly impugned the president's personal integrity. He did not send this letter.

To whom, or for what purpose you mean to apply the following words of your letter "I have been the meditated victim of party-spirit" will be found I presume, in your defence without which I shall never understand them. I cannot conceive they were aimed at me, because an hundred and an hundred times you have heard me lament from the bottom of my Soul that differences of sentiments should have occasioned those heats which are disquieting a country, otherwise the happiest in the world, and you have heard me express the most ardent wish that some expedient could be devised to heal them. . . . I do not write from a desire to obtain explanations; for it is not my meaning nor shall I proceed any farther in discussions of this sort, unless necessity should call for a simple, and candid statement of the business, to be laid before the public.[19]

> He despaired of administering to a nation diseased by party spirit. By spring 1796, a dejected Washington saw little hope.

I am *Sure* the Mass of Citizens in these United States *mean well*, and I firmly believe they will always *act well*, whenever they can obtain a right understanding of matters; but in some parts of the Union, where the sentiments of their delegates and leaders are adverse to the Government and great pains are taken to inculcate a belief that their rights are assailed, and their liberties endangered, it is not easy to accomplish this; especially, as is the case invariably, when the Inventors, and abetters of pernicious measures use infinitely more industry in disseminating the poison, than the well disposed part of the Community to furnish the antidote.[20]

> He had wearied of Cabinet infighting as well as newspaper sniping that cost friendships as well as peace of mind. When Jefferson disclaimed criticism attributed to him, Washington left no doubt that he was fed up with attacks on his integrity.

As you have mentioned the subject yourself, it would not be frank, candid, or friendly to conceal, that your conduct has been represented as derogatory from that opinion *I* had conceived you entertained of me. That to your particular friends and connextions you have described, and they have denounced me, as a person under a dangerous influence; and that, if I would listen *more* to some *other* opinions, all would be well. My answer invariably has been, that I had never discovered any thing in the conduct of Mr. Jefferson to raise suspicions, in my mind, of his insincerity; that if he would retrace my public conduct while he was in the Administration, abundant proofs would occur to him, that truth and right decisions, were the *sole* objects of my pursuit; that there were as many instances within his *own* knowledge of my having decided *against*, as in *favor* of the opinions of [Hamilton] evidently alluded to; and moreover, that I was no believer in the infallibility of the politics, or measures of *any man living*. In short, that I was no party man myself, and the first wish of my heart was, if parties did exist, to reconcile them.

To this I may add, and very truly, that, until within the last year or two ago, I had no conception that Parties would, or even could go, the length I have been witness to; nor did I believe until lately, that it was within the bounds of probability; hardly within those of possibility, that, while I was using my utmost exertions to establish a national character of our own, independent, as far as our obligations, and justice would permit, of every nation of the earth; and wished, by steering a steady course, to preserve this Country from the horrors of a desolating war, that I should be accused of being the enemy of one Nation, and subject to the influence of another; and to prove it, that every act of my administration would be tortured, and the grossest, and most insidious mis-representations of them be made (by giving one side *only* of a subject, and that too in such exaggerated and indecent terms as could scarcely be applied to a Nero; a notorious defaulter; or even to a common pickpocket). But enough of this; I have already gone farther in the expression of my feelings, than I intended.[21]

Washington had already asked Hamilton to polish a rough draft Farewell Address. He included Madison's earlier draft. Washington told Hamilton he wished to rebut critics who had been attacking him personally since that time and to propose a program for renewing the ideals of the Glorious Cause.

My wish is, that the whole may appear in a plain stile; and be handed to the public in an honest; unaffected; simple garb. . . .

[Including Madison's draft] will serve to lessen, in the public estimation the pretensions of [Jefferson's] Party to the patriotic zeal and watchfulness, on which they endeavor to build their own consequence at the expence of others, who have differed from them in sentiment. And besides, it may contribute to blunt, if it does not turn aside, some of the shafts which it may be presumed will be aimed at my annunciation of this event; among which, conviction of fallen popularity, and despair of being re-elected, will be levelled at me with dexterity and keenness. . . .

My object has been, and must continue to be, to avoid personalities; allusions to particular measures, which may appear pointed; and to expressions which could not fail to draw upon me attacks which I should wish to avoid, and might not find agreeable to repel. . . .

As this Address, Fellow citizens will be the last I shall ever make you, and as some of the Gazettes of the United States have teemed with all the Invective that disappointment, ignorance of facts, and malicious falsehoods could invent, to misrepresent my politics and affections; to wound my reputation and feelings; and to weaken, if not entirely destroy the confidence you had been pleased to repose in me; it might be expected at the parting scene of my public life that I should take some notice of such virulent abuse. But, as heretofore, I shall pass them over in utter silence; never having myself, nor by any other with my participation or knowledge, written, or published a scrap in answer to any of them.

My Politicks have been unconcealed; plain and direct. They will be found (so far as they relate to the Belligerent Powers) in the Proclamation of the 22d of April 1793; which, having met your approbation, and the confirmation of Congress, I have uniformly and steadily adhered to, uninfluenced by, and regardless of the complaints and attempts of *any of those* powers or their partisans to change them.

The Acts of my Administration are on Record. By these, which will not change with circumstances, nor admit of different interpretations, I expect to be judged. If they will not acquit me, in your estimation, it will be a source of regret; but I shall hope notwithstanding, as I did not seek the Office with which you have honored me, that charity may throw her mantle over my want of abilities to do better; that the gray hairs of a man who has, excepting the interval between the close of the Revolutionary War, and the organization of the new government either in a civil, or military character, spent five and forty years, *All the prime of his life*, in serving his country, be suffered to pass quietly to the grave; and that his errors, however, numerous; if they are not criminal, may be consigned to the Tomb of oblivion, as he himself soon will be to the Mansions of Retirement.

To err, is the lot of humanity, and never for a moment,

have I ever had the presumption to suppose that I had not a full proportion of it. Infallibility not being the attribute of Man, we ought to be cautious in censuring the opinions and conduct of one another. To avoid intentional error in my public conduct, has been my constant endeavor. . . .

It was not from ambitious views; it was not from ignorance of the hazard to which I knew I was exposing my reputation; it was not from an expectation of pecuniary compensation, that I have yielded to the calls of my country; and that, if my country has derived no benefit fom my services, my fortune, in a pecuniary point of view, has received no augmentation from my country. But in delivering this last sentiment, let me be unequivocally understood as not intending to express any discontent on my part, or to imply any reproach on my country on that account.

I retire from the Chair of government no otherwise benefitted in this particular than what you have all experienced from the increased value of property, flowing from the Peace and prosperity with which our country has been blessed amidst tumults which have harrassed and involved other countries in all the horrors of War. I leave you with undefiled hands, an uncorrupted heart, and with ardent vows to heaven for the welfare and happiness of that country in which I and my forefathers to the third or fourth progenitor drew our first breath.[22]

> Hamilton's revision reshaped that draft into a dignified presidential statement of principle that Washington then revised in his own words "to avoid the imputation of affected modesty" and "the appearance of self-distrust and mere vanity."[23] The final version totaled about 3 percent Madison's words, 73 percent Hamilton's, and the remainder Washington's. He himself proofread the final draft

before having it printed in Philadelphia's *American Daily Advertiser* on 19 September 1796.[24]

On 13 March 1797, he issued a final proclamation—this one pardoning leaders of the Whiskey Rebellion.

11

FINDING PEACE

4 MARCH 1797–14 DECEMBER 1799

At John Adams's inauguration, Washington in a black civilian suit and a military hat strode to his seat quickly, thus dampening applause as he entered Congress Hall. Adams reported the scene for the absent Mrs. Adams.

[A solemn scene it was indeed, and it was made affecting to me by the presence of the General, whose countenance was as serene and unclouded as the day. He seemed to enjoy a triumph over me. Methought I heard him say, 'Ay! I am fairly out and you fairly in! See which of us will be happiest!'][1]

The Washingtons left in their chariot for a triumphal journey home on the 9th, along with two eighteen-year-olds, granddaughter Nelly and Lafayette's son George. His diary recorded a minimum of fussing or fetes.

[March] 9. Left Philadelphia on my return to Mt. Vernon.

12. Dined and lodged in Baltimore. Met and escorted into town by a great concourse of people.

14. Dined at Mr. [Thomas] Laws and lodged at Mr. Thomas Peters [both Mrs Washington's grandsons-in-law]. Day warm.

15. Received the Compliments of the Citizens of George Town as I had done the day before those of the City of Washington. Stopped in Alexandria and got to Mt Vernon to dinner.[2]

We got home without accident, and found the Roads drier, and better than I ever travelled them at that Season of the year. The attentions we met with on our journey were very flattering, and to some whose minds are differently formed from mine would have been highly relished; but I avoided in every instance where I had any previous knowledge of the intention, and could by earnest entreaties prevail, all parade or escorts. Mrs Washington took a violent cold in Philadelphia, which hangs upon her still, but not as bad as it did.

I find myself in the situation, nearly, of a young beginner, for although I have not houses to build (except one, which I must erect for the accomodation and security of my Military, Civil and private Papers, which are voluminous and may be interesting) yet I have not one, or scarcely any thing else about me that does not require considerable repairs. In a word, I am already surrounded by Joiners, Masons, Painters etc etc and such is my anxiety to get out of their hands, that I have scarcely a room to put a friend into, or to set in myself, without the Music of hammers, or the odoriferous smell of Paint.[3]

Washington's letters to intimate friends reflected the same lighthearted spirit—as in telling Secretary of War James McHenry he had no news from the country.

I begin my diurnal course with the Sun . . . if my hirelings are not in their places at that time I send them messages expressive of my sorrow for their indisposition—then having put these wheels in motion, I examine the state of things farther; and the more they are probed, the deeper I find the wounds are, which my buildings have sustained by an absence, and neglect of eight years.

By the time I have accomplished these matters, breakfast (a little after seven oclock, about the time I presume you are taking leave of Mrs McHenry) is ready. This over, I mount my horse and ride round my farms, which employs me until it is time to dress for dinner; at which I rarely miss seeing strange faces—come, as they say, out of respect to me. Pray, would not the word curiosity answer as well? and how different this, from having a few social friends at a cheerful board?

The usual time of sitting at Table—a walk—and Tea—brings me within the dawn of Candlelight; previous to which, if not prevented by company, I resolve, that as soon as the glimmering taper, supplies the place of the great luminary, I will retire to my writing Table and acknowledge the letters I have received; but when the lights are brought, I feel tired, and disinclined to engage in this work, conceiving that the next night will do as well; the next comes, and with it the same causes for postponement, and effect; and so on. . . .

Having given you the history of a day, it will serve for a year; and I am persuaded you will not require a second edition of it: but it may strike you, that in this detail no mention is made of any portion of time allotted for reading; the remark would be just, for I have not looked into a book since I came home, nor shall be able to do it until I have discharged my workmen; probably not before the nights grow longer; when, possibly, I may be looking in doomsday book.[4]

> In the same light-hearted spirit, Mrs. Washington sent
> their old neighbor Elizabeth Powel another jocular letter.
> She would often serve as copyist for him, but, as part of

the fun, this one was drafted by Washington then copied and signed as if by her.[5]

I am now, by desire of the General to add a few words on his behalf; which he desires may be expressed in the terms following, that is to say, that despairing of hearing what may be said of him, if he should really go off in an apopletic, or any other fit, (for he thinks all fits that issue in death—are worse than a love fit, a fit of laughter, and many other kinds which he could name)—he is glad to hear *before-hand* what will be said of him on that occasion; conceiving that nothing extra will happen between *this* and *then* to make a change in his character for better, or for worse. And besides, as he has entered into an engagement with Mr [Robert] Morris, and several other Gentlemen, not to quit the theatre of *this* world before the year 1800, it may be *relied upon* that no breach of contract shall be laid to him on that account, unless dire necessity should bring it about, maugre all his exertions to the contrary. In that case, he shall hope they would do by him as he would by them: excuse it. At present there seems to be no danger of his giving them the slip, as neither his health, nor spirits, were ever in greater flow, notwithstanding, he adds, he is descending, and has almost reached, the bottom of the hill; or in other words, the shades below.[6]

In what must have been seen another instance of *déjà vu*, sixteen-year-old George Washington Custis, like his father, dropped out of Princeton, then returned to school and found love. Besides chiding him for not writing ("knowing, as you must do, how apt your Grandmama is to suspect that you are sick, or some accident has happened to you") Washington lectured him on the relative merits of education and love.

We have, with much surprise, been informed of your devoting much time, to paying particular attentions to, a certain young lady [Elizabeth Jennings of Annapolis]. Knowing that conjectures are often substituted for facts, and idle reports are circulated without foundation, we are not disposed to give greater credit to *these* than what arises from a fear that your application to *Books* is not such as it ought to be; and that the hours which might be more profitably employed at studies are misspent in this manner.

Recollect the saying of the wise man, "That there is a time for all things" and sure I am it is not a time for you to think of forming a serious attachment of this kind, and *particular* attentions without, this would be dishonourable and might involve a consequence of which you are not aware.

In forming a connection, which is to be binding for life, many considerations, besides the mere gratification of the passions, and of more durability, are essential to happiness. These, in a *boy* of your age, all yield to the latter; which, when endulged, too often fleets away, and when it is too late, the others occur with sorrow and repentance.[7]

> Young Custis returned home to Mount Vernon. Disappointed that he had dropped out of school again, Washington posted a list of groundrules that at times sounded like the rules of propriety copied in his own childhood but now with added comments on their utility.

• System in all things should be aimed at; for in execution, it renders every thing more easy.

• If now and then, of a morning before breakfast, you are inclined, by way of change, to go out with a Gun, I shall not object to it; provided you return by the hour we usually set down to that meal.

• From breakfast, until about an hour before Dinner

(allowed for dressing, and preparing for it, that you may appear decent) I shall expect you will confine yourself to your studies; and diligently attend to them; endeavouring to make yourself master of whatever is recommended to, or required of you. . . .

· Rise early, that by habit it may become familiar, agreeable—healthy—and profitable. It may for a while, be irksome to do this; but that will wear off; and the practise will produce a rich harvest forever thereafter; whether in public, or private Walks of Life.

· Make it an invariable rule to be in place (unless extraordinary circumstances prevent it) at the usual breakfasting, dining, and tea hours. It is not only disagreeable, but it is also very inconvenient, for servants to be running here, and there, and they know not where, to summon you to them, when their duties, and attendance, on the company who are seated, render it improper.

· Saturday may be appropriated to riding; to your Gun, or other proper amusements.

· Time disposed of in this manner, makes ample provision for exercise & every useful, or necessary recreation; at the sametime that the hours allotted for study, *if really applied to it*, instead of running up and down stairs, and wasted in conversation with any one who will talk with you, will enable you to make considerable progress in whatsoever line is marked out for you.[8]

> Both of the Washingtons renewed correspondence in May
> 1798 with Sally Fairfax, now widowed and living in
> England, reminding them all of happier days when she
> dwelt at Belvoir. While Mrs. Washington told her about
> changes in the neighborhood, he summarized the course
> of his career since they parted, and ended with allusions to
> ominous threats of invasion by Revolutionary France.

So many important events have occurred, and such changes in men and things have taken place, as the compass of a letter would give you but an inadequate idea of. None of which events, however, nor all of them together, have been able to eradicate from my mind, the recollection of those happy moments—the happiest of my life—which I have enjoyed in your company.

Worn out in a manner by the toils of my past labour, I am again seated under my Vine and Fig tree, and wish I could add that there are none to make us affraid; but those whom we have been accustomed to call our good friends and allies, are endeavouring if not to make us affraid, yet to despoil us of our property; and are provoking us to Acts of Self-defence, which may lead to War. What will be the result of such measures, time, that faithful expositor of all things, must disclose. My wish is, to spend the remainder of my days (which cannot be many) in rural amusements—free from those cares which public responsibility is never exempt.[9]

Keeping up with politics at home and diplomacy abroad, he grew increasingly troubled by France's aggression. She even sought bribes. In mid-July 1798 a frenzied public moved President John Adams to draft a reluctant Washington as commander-in-chief once more.

Little did I expect, when my valadictory address was presented to the People of the United States, that any event would occur in my day, that could draw me from the peaceful walks and tranquil shades of Mount Vernon; where I had fondly hoped to spend the remnant of a life, worn down with public cares, in ruminating on the variegated scenes through which I have passed—and in the contemplation of others which are yet in embrio. . . .

I might, in the course of events, be left with the single consolation of knowing *myself*, though, possibly, deprived even the credit of <u>that</u> by the malevolence of others, that a sense of duty was the *only* motive which had induced me to run the risk and to make the Sacrafice of my ease and quiet at the same time.[10]

> As French forces busied themselves elsewhere, public fervor flagged and so did enlistments. Washington spent November 1798 in Philadelphia formulating plans and attending galas in his honor while Hamilton served as his field commander. The time away from Mount Vernon was not entirely wasted. By December's end he was able to find a military niche for George Washington Custis.

A thorough conviction that it was a vain attempt to keep Washington Custis to any literary pursuits, either in a public Seminary, or at home under the direction of any one, gave me the first idea of bringing him forward as a Cornet of Horse. To this measure too I was induced by a conviction paramount in my breast, that if real danger threatned the Country, no young man ought to be an idle Spectator of its defense; and that, if a state of preparation would avert the evil of an Invasion, he would be entitled to the merit of proffered service, without encountering the dangers of War: and besides, that it might divert his attention from a Matrimonial pursuit (for a while at least) to which his constitution seems to be too prone.[11]

> The matrimonial event that gave him most pleasure was the marriage of Nelly Custis, his adopted granddaughter, to his favorite nephew Lawrence Lewis. They wed on Washington's birthday in 1799. He dressed in his old buff and blue uniform and hat with black cockade. His wedding gift was the neighboring farm that would keep them close to Mount Vernon.
>
> Meanwhile, he found pleasure in corresponding about

current events and politics. Discussing the shortage of housing for congressmen in the new Federal City, he quipped, "Oh well, they can camp out. The Representatives in the first line, the Senate in the second, the President with all his suite in the middle."[12]

He could also joke about more serious matters as allegations in the press that British spies had bribed the Adams administration. He teased his friend McHenry.

And pray, my good Sir, what part of the 800,000 dollars have come to your share?—As you are high in Office, I hope you did not disgrace yourself in the acceptance of a paltry bribe—a hundred thousand dollars perhaps.[13]

He firmly supported President Adams's repressing the opposition by restricting immigration and political criticism. But his life centered on his farms and Mount Vernon. Death of his brother Charles in September found him resigned to his own mortality.

The death of near relations, always produce awful and affecting emotions, under whatsoever circumstances it may happen. That of my brother's has been so long expected, and his latter days so uncomfortable to himself, must have prepared all around him for the stroke; though painful in the effect.

I was the *first*, and am now the *last*, of my fathers Children by the second marriage who remain. When I shall be called upon to follow them, is known only to the giver of life. When the summons comes I shall endeavour to obey it with a good grace.[14]

Accustomed to careful preparation, he drew up a detailed will by himself, leaving his estate to Mrs. Washington as long as she lived. He wished the land other than Mount Vernon to be sold, setting a value to each parcel for a total of $500,000, some of which remained unsold for many years. The will provided that the 124 slaves he owned be freed after Mrs. Washington's death, but she freed them soon after he died. He could not legally free her so-called dower slaves. His last days followed the usual round of visiting farms and visiting with friends. On the 12th, he stayed in the saddle about five hours in chilling rain.

[December] 12. Morning Cloudy—Wind at North East & Mercury 33. A large circle round the Moon last Night. About 1 oclock it began to snow—soon after to Hail and then turned to a settled cold Rain. Mercury 28 at Night.

13. Morning Snowing & about 3 Inches deep. Wind at North East & Mercury at 30. Continuing Snowing till 1 Oclock and about 4 it became perfectly clear. Wind in the same place but not hard. Mercury 28 at Night.[15]

Probably suffering from a strep throat, he worked through the afternoon, read the newspaper aloud that evening, but woke about midnight in pain. The next day, a team of doctors bled him about seven times. Between ten and eleven at night, attended by Martha Washington, Dr. James Craik, his companion from frontier days, and secretary Tobias Lear, he "expired without a struggle or sigh." Lear recalled the scene.

[He said to me, "I find I am going, my breath cannot continue long; I believed from the first attack it would be fatal, do you arrange and record all my late military letters and papers—arrange my accounts and settle my books. . . ."

About five o'clock Dr. Craik came again into the room, and, upon going to the bedside the General said to him: "Doctor, I die hard, but I am not afraid to go. . . ."

Dr. Craik asked him if he could sit up in the bed. He held out his hand to me and was raised up, when he said to the physicians, "I feel myself going. I thank you for your attention. You had better not take any more trouble about me, but let me go off quietly. . . ."

About ten o'clock he made several attempts to speak to me . . . at length he said, "I am just going. Have me decently buried, and do not let my body be put into the Vault in less than three days after I am dead." I bowed assent for I could not speak. He then looked at me again, and said, "Do you understand me?"

I replied, "Yes, Sir."

"'Tis well," said he. . . .

Mrs. Washington who was sitting at the foot of the bed asked, with a firm and collected voice, "Is he gone?"

I could not speak, but held up my hand as a signal that he was.

"'Tis well" said she. . . .]¹⁶

Notes

For abbreviations, see "Sources" on page 153.

Introduction

1. Below, p. 70.
2. Zall, ed., *Franklin on Franklin* 111.
3. Morse 132; F 35:142n.
4. Adair and Schutz, eds. 15.
5. Jefferson, *Writings*, ed. Ford 1:203, 222, 254.
6. Abigail Adams 15.
7. Selections from Burges 201.
8. Below, p. 42.
9. For example, Jones 266; Custis 491, 492; Ames 1:568.
10. Quaife, Weig, and Appleman 26.
11. Higginbotham 74.
12. Huske 66.
13. Below, p. 26.
14. Pcol 1:119n.
15. Gordon 2:203.
16. John Adams 2:203.
17. Skeen 14.
18. Tallmadge 63–64.
19. Rush 330.
20. C.C. Proctor, ed., 257–58.
21. Jefferson, *Writings*, ed. Ford 7:100.
22. Morse 132.
23. *Letters of Members* 7:292.
24. McGuire 155–56.
25. Weld 164.
26. Perkins 199.

27. William Thornton letter, *National Intelligencer* (Washington, D.C.), 23 August 1823, 4:4.
28. F 1:xlvi.
29. Below, p. 110.
30. Pret 1:51–52.
31. F 16:116–17.
32. *Letters of Delegates* 6:323–25.
33. *Pennsylvania Gazette*, 21 November 1781; *Freeman's Journal*, 4 December 1781.
34. Below, p. 57.
35. Below, p. 80.
36. F 30:299.
37. Madison, "Detached Memoranda" 451.
38. de Kalb to de Broglie, 7 November 1778, number 1987.
39. Below, p. 89.
40. *Pennsylvania Packet*, 18 July 1787.
41. *Records* 3:302
42. Below p. 96.
43. Silverman 604–6.
44. Below, p. 100.
45. Burges 201.
46. [Findley] 100.
47. Dunlap 2:234–35.
48. Below p. 104.
49. Pprs 4:552.
50. Jefferson, *Writings*, ed. Ford 9:77–78.
51. "President Washington in New York" 499.
52. Scharf and Westcott 1:472–73.
53. Abigail Adams 70.
54. Ibid, 35.
55. Reprinted in Stewart, passim.
56. PTJ 26:603.
57. Griswold 305.
58. F 29:22–23; 33:475–76; 34:16–17.
59. F 34:17–18.
60. Madison, *Papers*, ed. Hutchinson, et al. 15:406.
61. F 33:476.
62. Ibid.
63. Link 194.
64. F 34:16.
65. Jay 4:197.

66. F 34:397.
67. Sedgwick to his family.
68. Hamilton 19:325n.
69. Below, p. 130.
70. Ibid.
71. Washington, *Farewell Address* 107, 135.
72. "Dwight" 26.
73. Stewart 533.
74. "Dwight" 48.
75. Twining 123; Custis 460n.; Svinin 34.
76. *Diaries* 6:131n.
77. Below, p. 30.
78. Ford 69.
79. Reed passim.
80. Strouse 610n; Tinker 719.

CHAPTER 1

1. Washington to Heard; Washington, *Writings*, ed. Sparks 1:546–49.
2. Humphreys 8.
3. Washington to Heard.
4. Moore, *George Washington's Rules.*
5. *Diaries* 1:6–23.
6. To Richard [1749–50], Pcol 1:44.
7. To Robin [1749–50], Pcol 1:41.

CHAPTER 2

1. Cleland 2–4.
2. Humphreys 9, 10.
3. Washington, *Journal* 2–20.
4. Gist 86.
5. Washington, *Journal* 20–23.

CHAPTER 3

1. *Diaries* 1:194–96.
2. Ibid., 196n.
3. Pcol 1:118.
4. *London Magazine*, 23 August 1754, 370–71; Mason 103.
5. Pcol 1:119n.
6. Ibid., 172.

7. Wallace, ed., 366–67.
8. Huske 66.
9. Pcol 1:168n.
10. Ibid., 226.
11. Ibid., 250.
12. Ibid., 256.
13. Ibid., 321–22.
14. Ibid., 343.
15. Ibid., 331.
16. Pickering 89–101; Humphreys 16–19; Pcol 5:520–23.
17. Davies 9n.
18. Pcol 1:352.
19. Loudon 25 January 1756.
20. Humphreys 21–22.
21. Humphreys 20–22.

CHAPTER 4

1. Pcol 6:11–12.
2. Ibid., 6:202.
3. Toner 20n.
4. *Diaries* 1:238.
5. Pcol 7:206.
6. Pret 4:467.
7. *Diaries* 1:276–77.
8. Royster, *Fabulous History* 103.
9. Pcol 8:2–3.
10. Pcon 1:93n-94n.
11. Pcol 8:301–2.
12. Ibid., 7:203–4.
13. Ibid., 228–29.
14. *Journals of the House* 313.
15. Pcol 7:395–96.
16. Ibid., 8:178.
17. Ibid., 89–90.
18. *Diaries* 2:68, 141.
19. Pcol 8:240, 360, 411; 9:219–20, 243.
20. Zall, *Founding Mothers* 18.
21. Pcol 10:234–35.
22. Ibid., 129.
23. Ibid., 155.

24. John Adams 2:117.
25. Pcol 10:172.
26. Ibid., 368.

CHAPTER 5

1. John Adams 3:323.
2. United States 2:92; Prev I:1.
3. Prev 1:3–4.
4. Martha Washington 164.
5. F 22:15.
6. Pcol 1:27.
7. Prev 1:335.
8. Zall, "American Jestbooks" 10.
9. Wright 125–26; Royster, *Revolutionary People* passim.
10. Prev 6:441–42.
11. Ibid., 5:534.
12. F 16:116–17.
13. Prev 2:296n.
14. Thacher 60–61.
15. Prev 5:408–9.
16. Ibid., 7:454.
17. See above, p. 34; Humphreys 21–22.
18. Prev 11:551.
19. F 12:156–57.
20. Varlo 2:90.
21. Van Doren 349–50.
22. F 21:62.
23. Ibid., 319–20.
24. *Diaries* 3:404.
25. Pcon 6:414–15.
26. F 23:340.

CHAPTER 6

1. F 25:269.
2. Ibid., 288.
3. Pcon 4:212.
4. F 26:214.
5. Skeen 14.
6. F 26:245–46.
7. Ibid., 486–96.

8. Ibid., 335–36.
9. Ibid., 27:190.
10. Ibid., 26:44–45.
11. Pprs 4:33–34.
12. F 26:39.
13. F 27:285.

<h2>CHAPTER 7</h2>

1. Pcon 1:87–88.
2. Ibid., 137–38.
3. *Pennsylvania Gazette*, 21 November 1781.
4. *Pennsylvania Magazine of History and Biography*, 17 (1893): 76–79.
5. Pcon 3:487–88.
6. Ibid., 2:415.
7. Ibid., 414–15.
8. Ibid., 1:235.
9. Ibid., 2:197.
10. Ibid., 4:52.
11. Decatur, February 1937, 4–5; March 1937, 5, 18–19.
12. Stuart 367–74.
13. Zall, *Washington Laughing* 10.
14. Watson 139. Watson adds: "These are nearly the words of Washington."
15. Réau 405.
16. Pcon 4:183–84.
17. *Diaries* 4:57–58.
18. Ibid., 174.
19. Humphreys 78.
20. Pcon 4:16.
21. Jefferson, *Writings*, eds. Lipscomb and Bergh 17:401.
22. Pcon 3:447.
23. Ibid., 4:212–13.
24. Ibid., 318.
25. Pprs 2:161.
26. Pcon 5:222.

<h2>CHAPTER 8</h2>

1. Pcon 5:238.
2. Ibid., 279–80.

3. *Diaries* 5:179.
4. Ibid., 183.
5. Pierce, "On the Federal Convention of 1787" 324–25.
6. *Diaries* 5:185.
7. Hunt and Scott 570.
8. Pcon 5:441.
9. *Diaries* 5:186.
10. Pcon 5:339.
11. Zall, "Corrigendum" 321.
12. Pcon 6:447–48.
13. *Records* 4:75.
14. Pprs 1:71–72.
15. Hellman.
16. Pprs 1:440.
17. Ibid., 200.
18. Ibid., 425.
19. Ibid., 2:2.
20. Ibid., 1:263.
21. Ibid., 368.
22. Ibid., 279–80.
23. *Diaries* 5:445.

CHAPTER 9

1. Martha Washington 276.
2. F 34:41–42.
3. Pprs 2:60.
4. Ibid., 108.
5. *Diaries* 5:447.
6. Pprs 1:339.
7. Maclay 13.
8. Pprs 2:160–64.
9. Pprs 2:246–47.
10. Pprs 5:526.
11. Pprs 2:390.
12. *Diaries* 5:453.
13. Ibid., 475–76.
14. *Philadelphia General Advertiser,* 23 April 1791, 2.
15. Pprs 8:265–66.
16. Pprs 9:130–31.
17. *Diaries* 6:107, 112, 114, 168.

18. Pprs 8:382–83.
19. Hamilton 12:277.
20. Jefferson, *Papers* 25:155.
21. Madison, *Papers,* eds. Rutland and Mason 14:310–12.
22. Freeman 6:336.
23. F 32:136–37.

CHAPTER 10

1. F 32:310.
2. Ibid., 448–49.
3. Jefferson, *Papers* 26:602–3.
4. Ibid., 26:627–28; 630.
5. Lycan 231.
6. 11 April 1794.
7. F 33:23–24.
8. Ibid., 479.
9. Ibid., 34:99–100.
10. Ibid., 89–90.
11, Ibid., 91–92.
12. Ibid., 33:501.
13. Moore, *Family Life* 108–9.
14. Zall, *Wit and Wisdom* 86.
15. Scott, ed. 244.
16. Quoted by Mary Anne Randolph Custis (Mrs. Robert E.) Lee in the prefatory memoir of her father, George Washington Custis, 41–44.
17. *Diaries* 6:182; 185; 193.
18. F 34:256.
19. Ibid., 344–45.
20. Ibid., 35:37.
21. Ibid., 119–20.
22. Ibid., 49, 50, 60–61.
23. Washington, *Farewell Address* 107, 135.
24. Ibid., 291.

CHAPTER 11

1. Freeman 7:437.
2. *Diaries* 6:236–39.
3. Pret 1:71.
4. Ibid., 159–60.

5. Ibid., 84n; 521n.
6. Ibid., 520.
7. Ibid., 2:324–25.
8. Ibid., 4–5.
9. Ibid., 272.
10. Ibid., 382; 512–13.
11. Ibid., 3:298.
12. Zall, *Wit and Wisdom* 87–88.
13. Ibid., 88.
14. Pret 4:318.
15. *Diaries* 6:378–79.
16. Washington, *Writings,* ed. Ford 14:249–50.

SOURCES

For readers' convenience in finding the extracts in fuller context, source notes refer to printed texts readily available in the ongoing edition, *Papers of George Washington*, edited by W.W. Abbot, et al., for the University of Virginia Press since 1983. The notes abbreviate subtitles of the five pertinent series: Colonial (**Pcol**), Revolutionary War (**Prev**), Confederation (**Pcon**), Presidential (**Pprs**), and Retirement (**Pret**). For texts not yet published in these series, the reference is to *Writings of George Washington* (abbreviated **F**), edited by John C. Fitzpatrick for the Washington Bicentennial Commission in thirty-nine volumes (1931–44). For extracts from Washington's diaries, the source is the edition by Donald Jackson and Dorothy Twohig in six volumes for the University of Virginia Press (1976–79) abbreviated *Diaries*.

Adair, Douglass, and John Schutz, eds. *The Spur of Fame*. San Marino, Calif.: Huntington, 1966.

Adams, Abigail. *New Letters of Abigail Adams, 1788–1801*. Edited by Stewart Mitchell. Boston: Houghton-Mifflin, 1947.

Adams, John. *Diary and Autobiography of John Adams*. Edited by Lyman Butterfield, et al. 4 vols. Cambridge: Harvard University Press, 1961.

Ames, Fisher. *Works of Fisher Ames*. Edited by William B. Allen. Indianapolis: Liberty Classics, 1983.

Brighton, Ray. *The Checkered Career of Tobias Lear*. Portsmouth, N.H.: Marine Society, 1985.

Burges, James Bland. *Letters and Correspondence of Sir James Bland Burges*. Edited by James Hutton. London: John Murray, 1885.

Cleland, Hugh. *George Washington in the Ohio Valley*. Pittsburgh: University of Pittsburgh Press, 1955.

Custis, George Washington Parke. *Recollections and Private Memoirs of Washington*. Edited by Benson J. Lossing. New York: Derby and Jackson, 1860.

Davies, Samuel. *Religion and Patriotism the Constituents of a Good Soldier*. Philadelphia: James Chattin, 1755.

Sources

Decatur, Stephen. "Washington Sits for His Portrait," *American Collector*, February 1937, 4–5; March 1937, 5, 18–19.

de Kalb, Baron, to Comte de Broglie, 7 November 1778. In *Facsimiles of Manuscripts in European Archives Relating to America 1773–1783*, edited by B.F. Stevens, number 1987. N.p., 1890.

Dunlap, William. *History of New Netherlands.* Vol. 2. New York: Carter and Thorp, 1840.

"Dwight, Jasper" [William Duane]. *A Letter to George Washington.* Philadelphia: the Author, 1796.

[Findley, William.] *Review of the Revenue System.* Philadelphia: Dobson, 1794.

Ford, Paul L. *The True George Washington.* Philadephia: Lippincott, 1896.

Freeman, Douglas Southall. *George Washington.* 7 vols. New York: Scribners, 1948–57.

Gist, Christopher. *Christopher Gist's Journals: With Historical, Geographical and Ethnological Notes and Biographies of His Contemporaries.* Edited by William M. Darlington. Pittsburgh: Weldin, 1893.

Gordon, William. *History of the United States.* Vol. 2. London: the Author, 1788.

Griswold, Rufus W. *The Republican Court.* New York: Appleton, 1855.

Hamilton, Alexander. *Papers of Alexander Hamilton.* Edited by Harold C. Syrett and Jacob E. Cooke. 27 vols. New York: Columbia University Press, 1961–87.

Hellman, George S. "Irving's Washington and an Episode in Courtesy," *Colophon* 1, no. 1 (1930): n.p.

Higginbotham, Don. *George Washington and the American Military Tradition.* Athens: University of Georgia Press, 1985.

Humphreys, David. *David Humphreys' Life of General Washington: With George Washington's "Remarks."* Edited by Rosemary Zagarri. Athens: University of Georgia Press, 1991.

Hunt, Gaillard, and James B. Scott. *The Debates of the Federal Convention of 1787.* New York: Oxford University Press, 1920.

Huske, John. *Present State of North America.* London: Dodsley, 1755.

Jay, John. *Correspondence and Public Papers.* Edited by Henry P. Johnston. Vol. 4. New York: Putnams, 1890.

Jefferson, Thomas. *The Papers of Thomas Jefferson.* Edited by Julian P. Boyd, et al. 29 vols. (ongoing). Princeton: Princeton University Press, 1950–.

———. *The Writings of Thomas Jefferson.* Edited by Andrew A. Lipscomb and Albert E. Bergh. Vol. 17. Washington, D.C.: Thomas Jefferson Memorial Association, 1903–4.

Sources

―――. *The Writings of Thomas Jefferson.* Edited by Paul L. Ford. 10 vols. New York: Putnams, 1892–99.

Jones, Joseph H. *Life of Ashbel Green.* New York: Robert Carter, 1849.

Journals of the House of Burgesses of Virginia 1761–1769. Edited by John P. Kennedy. Richmond: Virginia State Library, 1907.

Letters of Delegates to Congress. Edited by Paul Smith, et al. Vol. 6. Washington: Library of Congress, 1980.

Letters of Members of the Continental Congress. Edited by Edmund C. Burnett. Washington, D.C.: Carnegie Institution, 1921–36.

Link, Eugene Perry. *Democratic-Republican Societies 1790–1800.* New York: Columbia University Press, 1942.

Loudon, Lord (John Campbell). Notebook. MS LO 770. Huntington Library.

Lycan, Gilbert L. *Alexander Hamilton and American Foreign Policy.* Norman: University of Oklahoma Press, 1970.

Maclay, William. *Diary of William Maclay and Other Notes on Senate Debates.* Edited by Kenneth E. Bowling and Helen E. Veit. Baltimore: Johns Hopkins University Press, 1988.

Madison, James. "Detached Memoranda." Edited by Elizabeth Fleet. *William and Mary Quarterly* 3d ser., 3 (1946): 451.

―――. *The Papers of James Madison.* Edited by R.A. Rutland and T.A. Mason. Vol. 14. Charlottesville: University Press of Virginia, 1983.

―――. *The Papers of James Madison.* Edited by William T. Hutchinson, et al. Vol. 15. Chicago: University of Chicago Press, 1962–91.

Mason, Alfred B. *Horace Walpole's England.* London: Constable, 1930.

McGuire, Edward C. *Religious Opinions and Character of Washington.* New York: Harpers, 1836.

Moore, Charles. *Family Life of George Washington.* Boston: Houghton Mifflin, 1926.

―――. *George Washington's Rules of Civility.* Facsimile edition. Boston: Houghton Mifflin, 1926.

Morse, Jedidiah. *American Geography.* Elizabethtown, N.J.: J. Morse, 1789.

Perkins, Thomas Handasyd. *Memoir of Thomas Handasyd Perkins.* Edited by Thomas G. Carey. Boston: Little, Brown, 1856.

Pickering, John. "Washington's Narrative of the Braddock Campaign," *Essex Institute Historical Collections* 72 (1936): 89–101.

Pierce, William. "On the Federal Convention of 1787," *American Historical Review* 3 (1898): 324–25.

"President Washington in New York, 1789." *PMHB* 32 (1908): 499.

Sources

Proctor, C.C., ed. "After-dinner Anecdotes of James Madison," *Virginia Magazine of History and Biography* 60 (1952): 257–58.

Quaife, Milo M., M.J. Weig, and R.E. Appleman. *History of the United States Flag*. New York: Harpers, 1961.

Réau, Louis. *Houdon: Sa vie et son oeuvre*. Paris: F. Nobele, 1964.

Records of the Federal Convention of 1787. Edited by Max Farrand. 4 vols. New Haven: Yale University Press, 1911.

Reed, W.B., ed. *Original Letters from Washington to Joseph Reed*. Philadelphia: A. Hart, 1852.

Royster, Charles. *Fabulous History of the Dismal Swamp Company*. New York: Knopf, 1999.

———. *A Revolutionary People at War*. Chapel Hill: University of North Carolina Press, 1979.

Rush, Benjamin. *Letters of Benjamin Rush*. Edited by Lyman Butterfield. Princeton: Princeton University Press, 1951.

Scharf, J. Thomas, and Thompson Westcott. *History of Philadelphia 1609–1884*. Vol. 1. Philadelphia: Everts, 1884.

Scott, Kenneth, ed. *Rivington's New York Newspaper*. New York: New York Historical Society, 1973.

Sedgwick, Theodore. Letter to his family, 13 April 1796. HM 4758. Huntington Library.

Silverman, Kenneth. *Cultural History of the American Revolution*. New York: Crowell, 1976.

Skeen, C. Edward. *John Armstrong, Jr*. Syracuse: Syracuse University Press, 1981.

Stewart, Donald H. *The Opposition Press*. Albany: State University Press of New York, 1969.

Strouse, Jean. *Morgan American Financier*. New York: Random House, 1999.

Stuart, Jane. "The Stuart Portraits of Washington," *Scribner's Monthly* 12 (July 1876): 367–74.

Svinin, Paul. *Picturesque United States of America*. Edited by Avram Yarmolinsky. New York: W.E. Rudge, 1936.

Tallmadge, Benjamin. *Memoir of Col. Benjamin Tallmadge*. New York: Thomas Holman, 1858.

Thacher, James. *Military Journal during the American Revolution*. Boston: Richardson and Lord, 1823.

Tinker, Edward. "Whitewashing," *The Bookman* (New York) 60 (February 1925): 719.

Toner, Joseph M. *George Washington as Inventor & Promoter of Useful Arts*. Washington: Gedney & Roberts, 1892.

Sources

Twining, Thomas. *Travels in America a Hundred Years Ago.* New York: Harpers, 1894.

United States. Continental Congress. *Journals of the Continental Congress, 1774–1789.* Edited by Worthington C. Ford. Vol. 2. Washington: GPO, 1905.

Van Doren, Carl. *Secret History of the American Revolution.* New York: Viking Press, 1941.

Varlo, Charles. *Floating Ideas of Nature.* Vol. 2. London: N.p., 1784.

Wallace, Paul A., ed. *Conrad Weiser, Friend of Colonist and Mohawk.* Philadelphia: University of Pennsylvania Press, 1945.

Walpole, Horace. *Memoirs of King George II.* Edited by John Brooke. Vol. 2. New Haven: Yale University Press, 1985.

Washington, George. *The Diaries of George Washington.* Edited by Donald Jackson and Dorothy Twohig. 6 vols. Charlottesville: University Press of Virginia, 1976–79.

———. *George Washington's Rules of Civility.* Edited by Charles Moore. Boston: Houghton Mifflin, 1926.

———. George Washington to Isaac Heard, 2 May 1792. HM 21704. Huntington Library.

———. *Journal of Major George Washington (1754).* Introduction by Randolph G. Adams. Facsimile edition. New York: Scholars' Press, 1940.

———. *The Papers of George Washington.* Edited by William W. Abbot, et al. 41 vols. (ongoing). Charlottesville: University Press of Virginia, 1983– .

———. *Washington's Farewell Address.* Edited by Victor Hugo Paltsits. New York: New York Public Library, 1935.

———. "Washington's Narrative of the Braddock Campaign." *Essex Institute Historical Collections* 72 (1936): 89–101.

———. *The Writings of George Washington.* Edited by John C. Fitzpatrick. 39 vols. Washington: Washington Bicentennial Commission, 1931–34.

———. *The Writings of George Washington.* Edited by Jared Sparks. Vol. 1. Boston: American Stationers Company, 1837.

———. *The Writings of George Washington.* Edited by Worthington C. Ford. Vol. 14. N.Y.: Putnams, 1893.

Washington, Martha. *"Worthy Partner": The Papers of Martha Washington.* Edited by Joseph E. Fields. Westport, Conn.: Greenwood, 1994.

Watson, Elkanah. *Men and Times of the Revolution.* New York: Dana, 1857.

Sources

Weld, Isaac, Jr. *Travels through the States of North America.* London: Stockdale, 1799.

Wright, Robert K., Jr. *Continental Army.* Washington, D.C.: Center of Military History, 1983.

Zall, Paul M. "Corrigendum," *Early American Literature* 33 (1998): 321.

———. *Founding Mothers.* Bowie, Md.: Heritage, 1991.

———. *George Washington Laughing.* Hamden, Conn.: Archon, 1989.

———. "The Old Age of American Jestbooks," *Early American Literature* 15 (1980): 10.

———. *Wit and Wisdom of the Founding Fathers.* Hopewell, N.J.: Ecco, 1996.

———, ed. *Franklin on Franklin,* Lexington: University Press of Kentucky, 2000.

———, ed. *Jefferson on Jefferson.* Lexington: University Press of Kentucky, 2002.

INDEX

Adams, Abigail, viii, xv, 132
Adams, John, viii, x, xii; at
   Contintental Congress, 52;
   inauguration of, xix; as
   president, 132, 138, 140
Addison, Joseph, 8
agriculture. *See* farming
Alexandria, Va., 39, 94, 99, 133
Alliquippa, Queen (Indian
   leader), 22
American Daily Advertiser, 131
Andre, Maj. John, 62, 63
Arnold, Benedict, 62–63
Arnold, Peggy, 62–63
Athaws, Mr., 43
Aurora (newspaper), xix, 117

Bache, Benjamin Franklin, xix
Barbadoes, 9–12
Bassett, Fanny, 75, 98, 108
Bill of Rights, 90–91
blacks ("Negroes"), 40, 41, 54; in
   Barbados, 11, 12; colonists
   likened to, 49; as investment,
   42
Bonaparte, Napoleon, 46
Boston Tea Party, 49
Bowie, John, 77
Braddock, Gen. Edward, 28–29,
   30, 32, 33
Britain, xv, 3, 44, 49; in French

and Indian War, 78; raids on
   American shipping, 114, 117;
   war with revolutionary
   France, 110, 114, 115, 118,
   124–25
Bruff, Thomas, xi
Burges, Sir James Bland, xiv
Burgone, Gen. John, 61
Butler, Pierce, 92–93

Cabinet, xviii–xix, 105–6, 123,
   124–26
Cabot, Sen. George, xvii
Calvert, Nelly, 47
Campbell, John (Lord Loudon),
   33
Campbell, Maj. Andrew, 6
Canada, 13
Carter, Mr., 10
Cato (Addison), 8
Caunotaucarius ("the
   Towntaker"), 14
Charles III (king of Spain), 79
Clarke, Major, 10
Clinton, Sir Henry, 65
Concord, battle of (1775), 50
confederal government, 64, 68–
   69, 72
Congress, xi, xiv, 64; Continental
   Congresses, 50, 52; G.W.'s
   military career and, 56, 58, 63,

Index

Index

Fraunces Tavern (New York), 72
Frazier, John, 16, 22
Frederick County, Virginia, 41
Fredericksburg, Virginia, 42
French and Indian War, ix, 24–
36, 42
French Revolution, 114
Freneau, Philip, 115
Fry, Col. Joshua, 24

Gates, Gen. Horatio, 61
Gazette of the United States, 115
Genet, Edmond, 114
Gentleman's Magazine, The, 9
George II (king of England), ix,
26
George III (king of England),
xiv, 100
German settlers, 7
Gerry, Elbridge, 89
Gist, Christopher, 17, 20–21, 22,
63
Gordon, William, 77, 78
Grasse, Adm. François Comte de,
66
Greene, Gen. Nathanael, 61
Greene, Bell, xxi
guerrilla war, 25, 60

Half-King, the (Indian leader),
15, 16, 17, 19, 29; name for
G.W., 14; in war against
France, 24, 25–26, 27
Hamilton, Alexander, 57, 89, 114,
116, 139; conflict with
Jefferson, 111, 112, 115, 127;
G.W.'s Farewell Address and,
xviii–xix, 128, 130–31;
resignation from Cabinet,

117; as Treasury Secretary,
111; Whiskey Rebellion and,
123
Hancock, John, 106
Henry, Patrick, 50, 90
Hessians, 60
Hilary, Dr., 10
Holland, 115
Hopkinson, Francis, 97
Horse-Hoeing Husbandry (Tull),
40
Houdon, Jean Antoine, xii, 79,
80–81
House of Burgesses, 40, 44–45,
46, 50
Howe, Lord Richard, 58, 59, 66
Howe, Gen. Sir William, 58, 61–
62
humility, viii, x
Humphreys, David, x, 30
Hunter, John, 75–76

illnesses, 37
Indian tribes, 6–7, 118–19; in
American Revolution, 67;
French influence among, 14,
15–17, 19–20, 24–27; frontier
tensions with, 41, 110, 112–
13, 114; U.S. federal treaties
with, 105

Jackson, William, 89
Jay, John, xvi, xvii, 104, 117
Jay treaty, xv, 117, 125
Jefferson, Thomas, xiv, xv, 83,
104, 114, 116–17; conflict
with Hamilton, 111, 112, 115;
Francophilia of, 117, 118, 124;
friction with Washington,

Index

Index